# Starting
# Your Career
## *as a*
# Freelance
# Editor

# Starting Your Career

## *as a*

# Freelance Editor

A GUIDE TO WORKING WITH AUTHORS, BOOKS,
NEWSLETTERS, MAGAZINES, WEBSITES, AND MORE

## BY MARY EMBREE

**ALLWORTH PRESS**
NEW YORK

Allworth Press books may be purchased in bulk at special discounts for sales promotion, corporate gifts, fund-raising, or educational purposes. Special editions can also be created to specifications. For details, contact the Special Sales Department, Allworth Press, 307 West 36th Street, 11th Floor, New York, NY 10018 or info@skyhorsepublishing.com.

15 14 13 12 11 5 4 3 2 1

Published by Allworth Press,
an imprint of Skyhorse Publishing, Inc.
307 West 36th Street, 11th Floor, New York, NY 10018.

Allworth Press® is a registered trademark of Skyhorse Publishing, Inc.®, a Delaware corporation.

www.allworth.com

Cover design by Jane Sheppard

Library of Congress Cataloging-in-Publication Data

Embree, Mary,
   Starting your career as a freelance editor : a guide to working with authors, books, newsletters, magazines, websites, and more / by Mary Embree.
      pages cm
   Includes bibliographical references and index.
   ISBN 978-1-58115-890-8 (pbk.)
   1. Editing—Vocational guidance. I. Title.
   PN162.E43 2012
   808.02'7023—dc23
                                    2011048747

Printed in the United States of America

# Contents

# Introduction

If you ever considered a freelance career as an editor, there probably couldn't be a more auspicious time to launch it than now. It has become a do-it-yourself world full of opportunities for creative and capable people who are also entrepreneurs.

In this age of economic uncertainty there are fewer traditional publishers of books, newspapers, magazines, and other periodicals than there were just a few years ago. Many existing publishers are issuing fewer paper copies and more people are getting their news and information online. But in most cases, the online publications contain just as many articles as they did when paper issues of these publications were being circulated. Some of the online copies of each issue carry a lot more information than their paper-only issues did. And all of those words have to be edited.

To cut down on costs publishers are hiring fewer in-house editors. And that opens up the field for freelancers. As we are independent contractors, we don't take up desk space in the office. Employers don't have to pay us for sick days or provide us two-week (or longer) vacations. All of that down time when we are not productive doesn't cost an employer a penny.

In addition to publishers, there are many small businesses and organizations that need the services of freelance editors, as well as departments in large companies. The material could be proposals, manuals, and catalogs. Individuals also need editors for career-enhancement writing such as résumés, dissertations, and term papers. They may also want our services for their more personal writing such as family histories and memoirs.

Although this book focuses more on book editing than on other kinds of editing, the principles are the same. No matter what field you are working in, you not only have to know what is standard for that specific genre and style but you must keep up to date on the changes that frequently occur in styles, spelling, punctuation, format, and so forth. As you will most likely be working directly with the author even when you are being paid by a publisher, your services will be most valuable if you can spot areas of change that your author has missed or doesn't even know about.

Editing is not just about correcting a manuscript, it is about guiding an author toward the completion of a first-rate professional piece of work. He or she will get the accolades while you, the editor, will fade into the background. And that is as it should be. After all, the author is the creator, the editor only helps to shape it and make it shine. However, without a qualified editor, many authors would never get published. Our work is vitally important.

There has been enormous growth in the number of low-priced books created by small publishers and self-publishers, some of whom have published only one book. And it is through working directly with authors and independent publishers that the freelance editor can flourish. It seems like almost everyone is writing a book or thinking about it.

There is a plethora of so-called self-publishing companies who help authors in every aspect of producing and selling their books. Many of these companies also provide editing services. However, in most cases editing is the weakest link in their chain of services. And that is unfortunate because it is the most important factor in producing a high-quality book. If a book isn't professionally edited according to book publishing standards it becomes immediately apparent to the reader that the publisher is an amateur, which results in the author losing much of his or her credibility as well as potential sales.

There are many different kinds of writing that need the magic touch of a good editor. In addition to books there are articles, dissertations, brochures, reports, abstracts, editorials, speeches, reviews, ad copy, and many more.

In writing this book I did a great deal of research on other editors in various fields, and learned that they came into the profession through very different pathways. Few of them set out to become editors and fewer still expected to end up working for themselves—and making a living at it!

Even so, most of them always knew that they could be editors. Like any art, editing requires both talent and craftsmanship. A good editor possesses not only training but an innate ability, a keen eye, and excellent language skills—all attributes that are capable of turning ordinary writing into something extraordinary.

All writers who want their work to look professional need an editor, whether they realize it or not. Even though I am a published author and have been a freelance editor for nearly twenty years, I can't always see my own mistakes. I'm just not that objective about my writing. Too many things can go wrong, from grammatical errors and repetition to inconsistent styles. Like all writers, I sometimes overlook the error because I know what I meant to write and my imagination sees it as it should be, not as it is. That's just human nature.

There is a difference between editing and proofreading but both have their place. A proofreader can come in very handy after the entire document has been edited. He will notice a missing word, too many spaces between words, typographical errors, and misplaced punctuation. It's always helpful for an editor to have a competent proofreader who can look over the final draft before it goes back to the writer or to the printer.

There are many different kinds of editing and many different kinds of documents. They all require specific expertise that can only be gained through training and experience. No one can be proficient in all of them. This book can't tell you what your particular path should be because there are too many ways to go. But you will learn what you need to know to decide on a specialty and where to research the information on how to get started. As you examine all of the advantages and disadvantages to becoming a freelance editor, you will be better prepared to make the decision: is this career meant for me?

# Ა 1 ᱔

## *Making the Choice*

Is editing the right career choice for you? If you find errors in just about everything you read; if you notice typos, misspellings, inconsistencies, redundancies, poor grammar, and bad punctuation; and if you have discovered mistakes in books by major publishers and wondered how they got past all of the editors who examined the text so carefully before it went to print, you just might be a natural editor. And if you have been accused of being a perfectionist or, worse, a nitpicker, well, congratulations! That's what it takes to become a *good* editor.

Editing can be as creative as writing. When we edit we must examine every facet of a manuscript, including the ease of reading it. In that way it is similar to writing. A fine editor goes far beyond catching errors. She must be knowledgeable about styles, genres, writing principles, organization, format, and appropriate language for the type of writing she is editing. She must know how to stay in the author's voice even as she makes corrections. Editing is providing the finishing touches, polishing, and bringing out the best a piece of writing has to offer. An outstanding editor might be called an alchemist—one who possesses a seemingly magical power of transmuting a common substance of little value into something of great value.

# THE DECISION TO BECOME AN EDITOR

How can you determine if a career in editing is right for you? There are a number of qualities you need to have to be a successful editor. Here are some questions to consider:

## Do you have the training and/or experience to do it well?

Like writing, editing is not easy. And anyone who thinks it is can't possibly be good at it. You must have an excellent command of the English language. You need a thorough knowledge of styles and you must have stylebooks used in the field of writing you are editing. You have to understand current publishing standards and have the ability to conform to those standards without changing the author's intent or voice.

## Do you enjoy editing?

H. G. Wells once said, "No passion on earth, neither love nor hate, is equal to the passion to alter someone else's draft." And I must confess that I am passionate about trying to make the writing the best it can be. The only job I like better than editing is writing.

Editing isn't always fun. Editing can be tedious, especially when we don't care for the subject matter. However, maintaining enthusiasm for the author's work is essential, if we are to do a good job for our client. When I am editing something that I don't find very interesting, I try to think of it as a word game. I enjoy crossword puzzles, word quizzes, and cryptograms and I like to think of the manuscript I am editing as that kind of intellectually challenging work. It helps to keep me interested.

Usually, though, I actually do enjoy the writing I am editing. I am constantly learning new things. When I edit how-to books I am getting an education and getting paid to boot. When I am editing a good novel, I am also being entertained. I love my job. But the most important thing I've gained, personally, by all the editing I have done is improvement in my own writing. Editing has definitely made me a better writer.

## Do you like detail work?

Editing takes a lot of concentration and the humility to acknowledge the fact that you don't know everything. You have to be able to determine when you need to check on something in the text, such as the spelling or definition of a word. You need to have the patience to examine every-thing about the manuscript from sentence structure to content and con-tinuity. You must look for such mistakes as too many spaces between words, a missing period at the end of a sentence or, as I have frequently noticed, more than one period. You must know when a title should be in italics and when it should be in quotation marks—and you have to be sure that whichever it is, it is consistent throughout the manuscript.

Because the English language is so eccentric, I always look up the spelling of words that I am not sure of. I think I am a good editor but, if I am, I believe it is partly because I realize that there are things I don't know—or can't remember. Then I go to a higher authority, such as *Webster's Unabridged Dictionary.* Not trusting my memory may show a lack of self-confidence, and I am quick to admit that I am not perfect. However, an over-confident editor is an editor who makes mistakes and doesn't even realize it.

## Are you comfortable working with writers?

The likelihood is that you will be working directly with the author at some point in the process. When your employer is the author you will be communicating with him on a regular basis. You must be able to relate to the author as a person, not just a client. Because I want the author to feel good about the process, I try to establish a comfortable working climate as well as a trusting business relationship. When you can think of your client as a friend and a partner you both will find the job more enjoyable. After all, both of you have good reasons to make the work the best it can be.

If on the other hand, you find that you have an immediate distaste for the material or lack of respect for the author, it's best not to take the job because that almost always signals trouble ahead. To continue under those circumstances is to do a disservice to both of you. Harold Ross, editor of *The New Yorker,* is quoted as saying, "Editing is the same thing as quarreling with writers—same thing exactly." Perhaps that is true for some editor/writer relationships but I don't like to work that way.

There is more about working with writers in another chapter.

## Are you willing to learn more about styles and genres?

Even when you are not getting paid to do research, you will need to learn new things to do your job well. When I am editing a novel, I buy (or borrow from the library) a recent bestselling book in the same genre as the one I am working on, such as a mystery, and read it in the evening when I am relaxing. I study how the author has set up his book, how he has foreshadowed events, where the climax and anticlimaxes are, and so forth. Although I will probably never write a mystery novel myself, I want to see how it is done when it is done well. It helps me to know what to look for in my client's book.

The same is true for any genre. If you are editing a self-help book, check out a few from the library and examine them to see the style the authors are using. There is a way of teaching, which self-help books seek to do, without preaching. For example, it is important for an author not to come across as being a know-it-all. Readers do not want to be talked down to as though the writer were preaching from a pulpit or standing on a pedestal. The author needs to place the reader on the same intellectual level as himself by frequently using words like "we" and "us" instead of "you" and "your." Here is an example of this from an excellent book titled *Emotional Comfort: The Gift of Your Inner Guide* that I edited for Judith Davis, MD, a noted psychiatrist and psychoanalyst.

> We have formed many habit patterns, some of which are very adaptive, others of which are less so. . . . We take them so for granted that even when they cause distress, it often doesn't occur to us that there may be other solutions.

Notice that she is talking about things we all do, including herself. As editors working with writers, we must be careful not to put ourselves on a pedestal. It is okay to say things like "You should avoid redundancies." But I suggest you also mention, "It's easy for writers to repeat sentences without realizing it. When we have rewritten our book a number of times we can't always recall saying the same thing in a prior paragraph." I often tell my clients that I have made the same mistake they made and that I am always grateful when my editor catches them. Some writers lack self-confidence about their writing and adverse criticism might discourage them.

Experience in other occupations can help you in your new career as an editor. Being a writer will help you be a better editor because you will have constantly confronted the need to be accurate, clear, and consistent in your own writing.

If you have done professional researching you will find editing much easier because you will know when and how to get important information that relates to that which you are editing.

And, of course, if you are a professional teacher you will find editing gratifying because you are also teaching the writer how to write better. You will be used to reading and grading your students' papers and showing them better ways to communicate.

So the message here is to use the experience you already have when you edit and look for ways to learn more. By constantly improving your knowledge you will become a more accomplished editor.

The examination of the above traits could help determine whether you are ready to launch your new career as an editor. And if not, you will have a better idea of what more you could learn to prepare yourself.

## THE DECISION TO FREELANCE

Is freelancing right for you? It certainly isn't for everyone. Starting a career as a freelance editor is similar to starting a new business where you are the sole proprietor. It takes more self-discipline to work for yourself than to have a regular job working for others. How many of the following questions can you answer in the affirmative?

### Are you a self-starter?

Not everyone can make a living freelancing no matter how intelligent or well trained they are. It takes a lot of self-discipline to get up early and get down to work each day even if your office is just a few feet away from your bedroom. And there are always things that must be done when you work for yourself. The rest of your life must be placed on hold while you are working. You can't run out to buy those shoes you saw on sale if you have a deadline for finishing the editing of a client's book, even if the shoes might be gone by the weekend. Your client must come first.

Working for yourself doesn't mean that you can take off whenever you feel like spending your precious time putting your golf club to the ball instead of putting your nose to the grindstone. If you don't want to devote five or six full days a week to doing your work, your days of making a good living as a freelancer may be far away. In real estate it is location, location, location. In freelancing it is discipline, discipline, discipline. Procrastination is the death knell to a freelance career. You can only put a client off for so long before that client starts looking for a more dependable editor.

### Are you good at time management?

One of the greatest challenges for freelancers is managing their time. With no one to tell you what to do, you must decide each day what your priorities are, set a schedule for yourself, and stick to it. You will have set aside the time to do the billable work necessary to generate an income. Unless you have a secretary, file clerk, and runner, you will have to do everything yourself.

Even if you have your office in your home and you have no small children who need your attention, there are always distractions. The dog wants out, the cat is climbing the screen to get in. The next-door neighbor wants you to feed her fish, water her plants, and pick up her mail while she's on vacation. After all, you are there all day every day. It wouldn't be inconvenient. Your best friend cut his hand while trying to fix the lawnmower and needs someone to drive him to urgent care immediately. He has no one else to call. Everyone else is at work— away from home in a real office. How can you say no? The sad fact is that when you work at home, no one thinks you are really working.

Friends call and want to chat in the middle of the day. You don't want to be rude to them but you find yourself constantly saying, "Can I call you tonight? I'm on a deadline." They reply as though rebuffed, "Well, I am so sorry I bothered you."

Time never seems to be on your side. Too often you have to decide between being a good friend and neighbor or making a living.

If you live in California and some of your clients are on the East Coast, you may have to get up earlier than you are used to—like around five in the morning—to call or email them. After all, five o'clock for you is eight o'clock for them and they have already started their day. And it's only two o'clock in the afternoon in California when it's quitting time in New York. If you choose to sleep late you might narrow that window of opportunity to reach an important client who could be gone for the day when you are just having your first cup of coffee.

### Are you well organized?

To make a good living freelancing you have to be well organized. If you are comfortable planning weddings, hosting a neighborhood barbecue, planning an itinerary, or forming a club or nonprofit organization, you must be a person who is well organized. You know how to plan and schedule an event, get people together, find a meeting place, order the catering, and all the other details necessary to pulling it off.

Freelancing is similar, except it isn't just an occasional happening, it requires organizing your personal life and business activities every day. It requires daily planning as well as long-range planning.

To keep track of all of my appointments, business and personal, I have a dry-erase board on the wall over my computer where I mark all of my upcoming activities for three months. As things change, I can update it instantly. You will probably find that making a list of all the things you need to do each day will help to keep you from missing deadlines and putting off some of the more boring tasks that you need to do. In my case, the boring tasks are filing and keeping my office organized. And I have to admit that I neglect them until it gets hard to find anything. That chore should go on your list at least one day a week.

At the top of my daily list are things that need to get done in the morning. Among them are making phone calls to New York and other cities where it is three hours later, working on manuscripts that have a deadline, answering emails, making appointments, and calling to confirm any appointments I have for that day. I reserve an hour for lunch and I put that on my schedule so I won't get caught up in work and forget to eat until my stomach starts to hurt. My afternoon is reserved for writing and editing. I schedule trips to the bank, post office, and office supply store for late in the afternoon. Often, when I have to go to the grocery store it is in the evening.

I go over my priorities in my mind at night just before I go to sleep. I think of the problems I need to solve and tell myself that I will work on those during the night as I sleep and then I will awake the next morning with the answers. This isn't just wishful thinking. I read recently that REM sleep is when we do our most creative thinking and problem solving.

Being well organized means being self-disciplined. Delaying gratification is tough but it is essential when you are a freelancer. Do you go out for a leisurely lunch with friends during your normal workweek or reserve that time for business meetings or doing research while you eat your lunch at your desk? When you are working for yourself, no one can fire you if you goof off. But you may find yourself unemployed anyway because when you freelance you don't get paid if you don't do the work.

## Can you spend the time needed to get your business started?

At the beginning, you must do a lot of planning, researching, and self-education to reach a point at which you are proficient at what you do. When you embark on this kind of career, you may not see a paycheck for quite a while. If you can't afford to pay your bills while you are developing your business, you might have to get a job elsewhere to cover your expenses. And it is hard to work for someone else while you are trying to get your freelance career off the ground. There are only so many hours in a day and you must take time to sleep, socialize, relax, and revitalize yourself.

When you are running an editing business, not all of the work you do every day is billable work. There is the job of maintaining your equipment, ordering office supplies, learning new computer programs, networking, paying bills, and doing paperwork such as keeping records of income and expenses. It all takes time.

If you want to avoid working elsewhere while you are developing your business, you might have to share an apartment with a friend or move in with your parents (or, if you are older, with your adult children) to cut down on living expenses. But a little family bonding might be beneficial for all of you. (Remember, I said "a little.")

If you have a spouse who is working, or well-heeled parents who will invest in your career, or income from investments, or an inheritance, this may not be a problem. Otherwise you might want to consider writing a grant or taking out a business loan to tide you over until your business is on a solid financial footing.

## Can you handle the down times emotionally?

In the best of all worlds, you would find a profession that pays well and only requires an hour or two of your time each day. However, we all live in the real world and the likelihood is that you will have to work more than a couple of hours every day to pay your living expenses. And to have some of the luxuries you would like, such as a new car or a vacation in Paris, you might even have to work (shudder) eight or more hours a day and more than five days a week.

Most likely there will be down times. That's the nature of almost all businesses, especially service businesses, such as editing and consulting. Even if you are still paying your bills on time you may occasionally see your savings account go down as you are tapping into it to cover living expenses. You may visualize losing your home, or having to sell your car, or any of a number of scary scenarios that you fear could occur in the not too distant future.

I will admit that even after twenty years of freelancing there have been slow times and I have spent some sleepless nights worrying about my financial future. However, I have always put aside enough money to carry me through three to six months without an income. And fortunately another editing job, a book deal, or a royalty payment has always come along before I've used up my emergency fund.

For a freelance editor—as well as a writer, which we all are in reality—there are usually other ways of bringing in money. And this is something nearly everyone who has talent, training, and experience possesses: the knowledge and ability to teach. Slow times can be filled with presenting writing seminars and workshops in your own community.

It almost seems as though there is a freelance gene built into some people that makes them persevere through difficult times. And whenever they think of throwing in the towel and getting a "real job" they realize that it is simply not an option for them. That was the case with me. When I worked for others I often felt like I had been sentenced to prison where I had to spend my time in a small enclosed space for eight hours every day taking orders from somebody else. It felt like I was being punished for something I didn't do.

In my last real job I had a large private office with a window but that didn't help a lot because when I looked out at the people walking around in the sunshine below I envied their freedom. That job lasted a year and I don't know whether I quit or was laid off. Those decisions seemed to have occurred simultaneously to both management and to me. They had to make staff cuts and I had come to the conclusion that the job just wasn't right for me. After several months of looking, I hadn't found another job and I was concerned. However, in a lucky coincidence, my unemployment insurance ran out at about the same time that I got my first freelance editing job.

Sometimes crises are blessings in disguise, because that's often when we become our most creative. It is the anxiety that accompanies the down times that forces us to expand our thinking. Worry can be a great motivator—it can trigger inspiration and lead us down a new and exciting path.

Being a freelancer can be unsettling at times, but if that is your calling you will probably find that no regular job will ever be exciting enough for you. And that attitude can spur you on to success.

## Do you have enough space in your home for an office?

Working at home is not only less expensive than renting an office, it also saves you on gasoline, lunches out, and business attire. If you can set up your office in a separate room, you may be able to deduct a portion of your rent or house payment from your taxes. You will probably also be able to deduct a portion of the utilities and a second telephone line. Having a home office saves time, too, because it won't take you very long to get from your bedroom to your office. Most people spend at least a half hour each way traveling to and from their job. That extra hour or more each day could be better spent working for your clients. And if you charge by the hour for editing, as I do, time really is money.

Although you might have to work at your dining room table in the beginning, having a spare room in which to set up your office is the ideal. You will have to get a computer, if you don't already have one, or you may have to buy a more up-to-date computer. You'll also need a printer, scanner, copier, and fax (preferably an all-in-one), a desk and chair, and of course you will also need office furniture.

Eventually you may want to lease office space but if you have the space in your home an outside office isn't necessary for the kind of work you will be doing. I prefer working at home. My friends know that I work full time and they don't usually call me until after five o'clock in the afternoon. When I feel the need to get up from my desk and take a ten-minute break, I can put clothes into the washing machine, refill the birdfeeder in my back yard, or take a brisk walk around the neighborhood. You can't do that when you have an office outside the home.

### If you have children, can you get child care when you get busy?

Another advantage to a home office is that, if you have school-age children, you will be there when they come home. You will be able to take them to doctor appointments and after-school activities.

However, when you have a family and there are small children to take care of, it may be difficult to work at home. It's easier if they are old enough to be in school because, during the school year you will have most of the day to yourself. If you want to work a full eight-hour day, you might want to consider sending your children to daycare or asking a friend or relative to take care of them after school hours.

An excellent option is to have your children go to the local Boys & Girls Club after school and for a few hours every day during the summer months. Having volunteered at several Boys & Girls Clubs, I think they are doing an outstanding job of keeping children safe, secure, and supervised. They also keep them interested and active in the Club's many activities that feature sports, arts, crafts, and educational programs. Being involved in a Boys & Girls Club is great for children whether they need supervision or not. It widens their horizons and provides opportunities for socialization they might not get otherwise.

Unattended children could either get into trouble or feel neglected. It would be hard to be a successful freelancer if you have to worry about your children's welfare.

### Are you willing to learn how to promote your services?

Like any business, promotion is the key to success. You may have depended on word-of-mouth to get editing clients at first. But you will have to get very creative in finding ways to promote your editing services because you will not be able to make a living unless you have a steady stream of paying clients to sustain you financially. Even if you are terrified of public speaking, you can overcome that fear by teaching a few seminars and workshops and, like me, you may soon find public speaking enjoyable. More and more often, I am invited to speak at book festivals, libraries, book clubs, bookstores, and other places where writers gather. That would be the likely outcome for you as well. Speaking engagements can bring in extra income and, even if you can't charge a fee for speaking at a library, you will be promoting your services. There is more on this in Chapter 4, Marketing Your Services.

## Are you willing to get additional training to update your skills?

The world we live in is constantly changing. Computers are obsolete after about two or three years, sometimes sooner. Word processing programs are always being updated and we have to buy a new one every few years. Then, if that isn't enough of a bother (and expense) we have to learn new ways to use them continuously. What we had gotten used to has been changed and nothing is in the same place it was in the old program. In fact, a lot of things are renamed and we have to learn a whole new vocabulary. Computers are a curse and a blessing. But like it or not, we must deal with them on their terms or the business world will pass us by.

There are classes you can take that will help you understand various kinds of programs you want to use. Check with your local community college for specialized training at low cost. There are instruction books both online and in print and it's a good idea to keep them close at hand so that you can look up things that you don't understand how to do.

This is not the kind of business where you can just rest on your laurels. Ongoing education and research are essential to your future success. You may find, as I did, that there are a lot of things you could do in addition to editing. When my clients asked me to recommend someone who could typeset their books and prepare them for printing, I learned how to do it myself. There was a natural progression from editing a manuscript to making it ready for publication. Now I am studying ways to help my author-clients promote and market their books. Internet promotion has exploded and I am learning about Facebook, blogging, websites, online newsletters, Amazon.com, eBay, and other ways to get the word out about my clients' books, as well as my own.

All of the matters mentioned above must be carefully considered before you begin. How you answer these questions could determine whether you will be able to make a living as a freelancer. But even if you didn't answer all of them in the affirmative, don't give up yet. There are some things you may be able to change about yourself, such as organizing and maintaining a consistent work schedule. And once you start making a little money, you may find that you no longer have to worry about self-discipline. Money is a great motivator.

## Do you know who your competition is?

Any writer with a computer can find an editor. They abound on the Internet. In the back of this book under Resources you will find a list of organizations and companies whose editor-members' services are available for hire. These editors and others in your own community are always looking for clients. They are your competitors. How does a writer choose among all of the editors available? How does the writer choose the right one for his work? It is not easy. Out of all of the choices, how will they find you?

You should learn as much as you can about other editors. Do a computer search to find other editors in your field. Find out what they specialize in and if they edit the same kinds of writing that you do. Check their websites on the Internet to learn how they promote their services. You will need this information to help you set yourself up as a specialist so that you can reach your target market and convince those writers to choose you and not someone else.

You might find that you would benefit by getting involved with one or more organizations. You may wish to get a listing on their websites that could drive more prospective clients your way.

## Is there a need for your services?

This is a question I can answer right here and now. Yes, there is. As Toni Morrison, novelist and editor, has been quoted as saying, "I cannot think of anybody who doesn't need an editor, even though some people claim they don't." More people than ever in history are writing books and publishing them themselves. More companies of all kinds are hiring freelance editors because it is too costly to keep editors on their payroll. Full-time employees must be paid benefits such as retirement and medical insurance. Freelancers are independent contractors. They don't cost companies as much as an employee would.

In the present economic climate, traditional publishers just aren't buying manuscripts that haven't been professionally edited. In an article for *The Writer* titled "An Editor Speaks From the Trenches," Peter Rubie wrote, "By and large, the novels we buy are 95% ready for publication. We don't have time to do much else with twenty-four or more books in production a year and reading on average two to three manuscripts a week, on top of all the line editing, conferences, and other work that has to be done."

Very few people have the qualifications to edit books or any other kind of writing. Being an English teacher is not enough, although it would help a great deal. As I stated before, editing is different in each field of writing. Specializing is essential if you are to become proficient because you can't know the standards or terminology for every kind of writing. But once you have acquired the skills at a professional level and have served a few clients who are very happy with your work, you have a good chance of getting good referrals and becoming known as an expert in your field.

## THE ADVANTAGES AND DISADVANTAGES TO FREELANCING

As you can see, there are both advantages and disadvantages to choosing the life of the freelancer. Here are a few of them.

## Advantages

- You are your own boss.
- You choose who you work for and the kinds of projects you work on.
- You set your own schedule.
- You could earn more for your services than you would if you were employed by a company.
- You don't have to please a supervisor.
- You get all the credit.
- You can't be fired, except by the individual client.
- You are doing what you enjoy, not what you have to do just to make a living.
- Your tax deductions are greater than they would be if you were working for someone else.

## Disadvantages

- It can be more stressful than working for somebody else.
- You won't get a steady paycheck.
- You may have to take out a loan to get started.
- You will have to furnish your own health insurance.
- You won't get sick leave or paid vacations.
- You won't get bonuses for good work. (But you may get repeat clients.)
- You will have to pay all of your own expenses.
- You have to buy your own office equipment and supplies.
- You must have space for your office furniture, supplies, and reference library.
- You will often work long hours.
- You will probably need legal advice and accounting services and they could be expensive.
- You may have to take a second job to cover the slow times.

## ADVANCED STUDY

So you've considered all of the above and you have decided that free-lance editing is the right career for you. You are ready to start establishing yourself as a professional editor. But there is one more thing you need to do before you embark on a career in editing. Be prepared. To do that you may want to consider some advanced study such as the following.

- Taking classes and workshops in editing
- Getting a degree in English
- Becoming an apprentice to an expert in your chosen field
- Working in the field as an assistant, intern, or volunteer
- Subscribing to journals, magazines, and newsletters in your field of interest
- Examining recently published novels, nonfiction books, textbooks, journals and other publications on subjects that interest you the most

# 2

## *Getting Started*

It probably isn't surprising to learn that most editors are also writers and many have even been published. Writing and editing go hand in hand. Experience as a writer will help you be a better editor and editing other people's work will enhance your own writing skills. As I interviewed freelance editors in various fields, I found that they reached that phase in their lives by very different pathways. The following are some stories of successful freelancers and how they got started. The first one is my story.

### HOW I GOT STARTED

Unlike most editors, I don't come from academia. I don't even have a degree in English. Much of my knowledge comes from on-the-job training, a lot of self-directed study, and many college-level classes to brush up on my English usage. In my younger years I worked as an executive secretary, usually for a department head or the CEO of the company. I wasn't hired for my typing speed or my ability to take short-hand. I wasn't very good at either of those. However, I could quickly edit and rewrite my boss's letters and reports to his satisfaction and that was more valuable to him because it saved him a lot of time. Unless a secretary is working with a person who is an excellent writer, and most executives are not, she also becomes an editor by default.

In my last executive secretarial position, I worked for the head of the Presentation Department at C. F. Braun, an engineering company. As engineers aren't generally noted for their writing skills, their letters and reports went through the Presentation Department to be "polished." My boss had been an English professor at the University of Southern California until C. F. Braun lured him away with a generous salary and benefits package. As there wasn't enough work for me to do as a secretary and I was bored, he decided to train me to be an "annotator," the term they used for what was actually an editor. He furnished me with college textbooks to study and suggested other books to read such as S. I. Hayakawa's *Language in Thought and Action,* which I read from cover to cover more than once.

For a year I was privately tutored by the former professor. He held regular staff meetings with the two annotators and me in which we discussed, and sometimes had heated arguments about, semantics. That is where I learned that a dictionary is not an authority—only a guide to the accepted usage as of that particular publishing date. A dictionary is actually obsolete, the former professor stated, the moment it is printed because definitions change very fast. For me it was a stimulating environment imbued with intellectual debates about the English language. That wealth of one-on-one training I received has served me well all these years. Unfortunately, I never did become an annotator. I got married and moved away before there was an opening in his department for that position.

Later, most of my jobs were in the entertainment field, mostly working in television production in various capacities from assistant to the producer to staff researcher and script editor. I also wrote scripts for the series *This is Your Life* and for independent producers of proposed TV shows. Because of that background, my focus is not only on writing principles and rules, it is also on making the writing interesting and, in some cases, entertaining.

For the past twenty years my career has focused on writing books and articles as well as editing books and doctoral dissertations. I do not edit poetry because I wouldn't want to mess with the author's style. I believe the poet's voice trumps standard writing principles.

Among the manuscripts I edit are novels, family histories, memoirs, and how-to and health-oriented books. Nearly half of my clients have been in the field of medicine, psychiatry, or psychology. Most of them were writing self-help books aimed at the general reader, such as dietary ways to control hormonal imbalance, a guide to permanent weight control, and psychological concerns of various kinds. There are certain genres of books I do not edit because I don't feel knowledgeable enough to do a good job. Among them are scientific journals or textbooks on subjects that require specialized training and are beyond my areas of expertise. In some cases, the editor of this kind of document must have a PhD or an MD degree.

If the writer-client is an expert who wants to write a book that will be accessible to readers who are not familiar with the jargon of his profession, that is a different matter. I will help her modify the language and presentation to make it more comprehensible—and interesting— to the average layperson.

My first freelance editing job was for a medical doctor and his nutritionist wife who were writing books on premenstrual tension and menopause. Neither considered themselves professional writers but they had important information they wanted to get across to women. As the book was aimed at female readers, not experts in the fields of gynecology or dietetics, they wanted someone who could take out the jargon and replace it with words and phrases that are readily understood by most readers. Thus, my lack of expertise in their disciplines was not a problem, it was a plus. Both of their books ended up being published by an imprint of Simon & Schuster.

In my second freelance job, working with a meteorologist, the situation was similar. When he asked me to edit his book I explained that I didn't know much about his field. He said, "That's exactly what

I need. This book is for anyone who is interested in weather and concerned about air pollution. I can't write for the general reader because I don't know what they don't know." As he explained it, scientific terms were part of his everyday vocabulary. He was concerned that he would write like a scientist and wouldn't be able to interest the very audience he wished to reach. He was concerned that he wouldn't even know when he was using a word that is not generally understood. As it turned out, he hadn't written much on the subject, which was air pollution, and I had to become a ghost writer, doing additional research and adding information to fill out the book that started with only twenty or thirty pages. Although I told him it was not required, he insisted on putting my name on the book as a cowriter. Since the subject was his and he had the ideas and the expertise in meteorology, we settled on "by Stephen E. Blewett with Mary Embree." It is generally understood in the publishing world that "by" indicates the author and "with" designates the person who did most of the actual writing. The title of the book was *What's In the Air: Natural and Man-made Air Pollution*. It was published several years ago and is currently out of print.

The above were cases in which I was hired for my ability to interpret esoteric ideas and information, and then transform them into readable language for readers at all levels of learning. I have since edited more than a hundred book manuscripts and dozens of dissertations, all as a freelancer. Editing books that educate, as many of the books I work with do, is a great way to learn a lot about interesting subjects.

My career as a freelance editor has been the most enjoyable job I have ever had. As a freelancer I can choose who I want to work for. If a client is difficult to work with, I suggest he find someone else and I bow out as graciously as I can. As I have many clients, when I am finished with a project it doesn't throw me out of work. I almost always have another client waiting.

Editing is not only enjoyable for me, it has helped me in my own writing. I have learned more from editing other people's books and dissertations than I could have learned through taking classes. And I have had the satisfaction of knowing that I helped many writers realize their dreams of getting published.

## HOW OTHERS GOT STARTED

The first story is Patricia Fry's. She helped me launch Small Publishers, Artists, and Writers Network (SPAWN) in 1996 and continues to run the nonprofit organization today, in addition to her writing and editing work.

### Patricia Fry's Story

In 1973 I started writing for publication and about ten years later I began supporting myself through magazine articles and books. Over the years, other authors often approached me asking if I would help them with their book projects. I always declined. I was able to generate so much of my own work that I had no interest in devoting time to theirs.

Eventually though, I caved. I tell people that I was forced into becoming an editor. In 1999 I edited my first book manuscript when an acquaintance with a fascinating true crime story finally broke through my self-imposed barrier against editing other authors' books. When the author asked me to edit it, I said yes—and I've been happily saying yes ever since.

I love editing. There's a sense of satisfaction in calming chaotic sentences, creating a better flow in a story, giving thoughts and ideas more power, discovering the real meaning in a disorganized presentation, and giving authors' messages more clarity. I delight in helping the author shine.

I have settled into a process of editing that takes me through the manuscript twice. While I used to do a once-over, I now realize how important that second editing is. As authors, we always read through our manuscripts many, many times before we consider it ready for publication—or to turn over to an editor. Editing is a process. I have discovered that the first edit offers me the opportunity to become familiar with the project. That's when I study the story/message and handle any obvious editorial problems. By the time I complete this process, I have made some decisions that might affect the earlier portions of the story or message. Sometimes an author has a writing style that fits the project and, rather than try to change it, I decide to help him enhance it. This type of decision cannot be made until you've delved into the manuscript a bit.

Amazingly, since I began editing manuscripts twice, my fees (I charge by the hour) have remained the same. Since I know I will be going over the material again, I may not ponder a problem for as long during the first go-round.

When potential clients contact me for the first time, I ask them to send me the word count for their manuscript, a table of contents (for a nonfiction book), and about thirty pages of the manuscript. I give them an estimate based on this material and information. I tend to push it up a bit in case I run into problems I don't foresee. And I love it when I come in under the estimate.

I am a teaching editor. I do not use the computer program's mark-ups. I edit on the computer, leaving the original text and punctuation intact and indicating the proposed changes in red. I also write notes to the author offering suggestions for future writings. When I come across a sentence I do not understand, I might ask the author to clarify rather than spending my time and their money trying to do it myself. If I can, I will offer suggestions.

Since I am also an author and publisher, I am in a position that many editors are not: I can provide sound publishing advice. In the case of a book proposal, I will explain to an author what is missing, what needs to be enhanced, and how he or she can make a stronger case for the book or for the platform, for example.

I don't write fiction, so I was concerned that I would not be able to edit fiction. I've discovered, however, that I actually have a knack for editing fiction and find it quite satisfying. The problems I commonly see in nonfiction manuscripts occur in fiction, as well. However, there are additional concerns such as the way the story is presented (show, don't tell), inconsistencies (if you change the story make the changes throughout), developing and maintaining believable characters, and so forth.

I believe that editing is a skill, but also an art-form. I have always enjoyed the editing process when it came to my own material. I'm so glad that I developed the courage to edit that first client manuscript. Since then, I have edited something like fifty or sixty manuscripts and dozens of book proposals.

Do I ever turn down editing jobs? You bet your life, I do. There have been a handful of authors that I sent back to the drawing board. They were nowhere near ready to be edited. My advice to these writers was to join a writers' critique group. Read their material and listen carefully to what others say. Read books like the one you want to write. And practice, practice, practice.

*Patricia Fry is an author, editor, and the Executive Director of Small Publishers, Artists & Writers Network (SPAWN). Contact information: www.spawn.org; www.matilijapress.com; www.patriciafry.com; PLFry620@yahoo.com*

Next is the editing history of a man I met when we were serving jury duty. We were the first two prospective jurors to be excused during jury selection and as we left the courthouse we met and spoke briefly in the parking lot. Neither of us could figure out what we said or did that kept us from being chosen as jurors. However, we discovered that we had something else in common. Both of us were freelance editors. Maybe that was it. Did they think that someone in such an exacting profession would be too opinionated to be an impartial judge? We'll never know.

At any rate, since I had just gotten the contract from Allworth to write this book, I took the opportunity to ask him if he would be willing to tell how he got started as a freelance editor. Fortunately, he said he'd be happy to. His is a fascinating story about a type of editing that is very different from what I do—and yet the same principles apply. Here is Bruce's experience in his own words.

## Bruce Novotny's Story

I received my college degree in English from the University of Notre Dame and I had a brief stint post-grad at the University of Cambridge. For several years after college I worked at the family business, a marina, and did some writing for a local weekly on Long Beach Island, New Jersey. During that time I wrote a novel that was later published by a small local publisher.

When I moved to Southern California I had no discernible career skills aside from the ability to put words on paper and have them make a little bit of sense. So in 1996 I responded to an ad from an advertising agency in Malibu, looking for seasonal help. It was a political ad agency and we were heading into a presidential election campaign season. I helped to place media and then was kept on after the campaign ended, to learn the Avid and provide some relief to their overworked senior editor. My background in writing helped me, to be sure, but it had little to do in a practical sense with the demands of the job. Editing text is a completely different field from editing film or video. Both are, in their own way, storytelling but with text you are manipulating the written word. With film and video you are working with essentially a moving visual image, although the spoken word— any aural element such as music or ambient sound—is a very powerful component as well, and easily overlooked.

The Avid is a computer software and hardware system that allows moving images, whether film or video, to be converted to digital information and arranged. Although some directors still prefer to cut on film, Avid has become the standard editing tool for features and television.

The ad agency was a nationally renowned shop that had its own Avid system and digital tape output equipment, so that we could finish TV spots and output them directly to broadcast outlets. They trained me on the equipment and when the senior editor moved on a few years later, I took over the whole department.

That company was bought by a prominent PR corporation and the Malibu office, being really expensive to operate, was closed. I was cast adrift into the freelance world with modest skills and experience, and little confidence. Work was difficult to come by, since relationships are the currency of that world and, being locked away in Malibu, I'd had few opportunities to build a network of industry contacts. I was able to secure a couple of steady clients through industry job-hunting websites like mandy.com, and one of my colleagues at the old agency led me to a very rewarding, long-term relationship with another client, a relationship that continues to this day.

I have reached the stage in my career where I have a healthy network of people with whom I've worked in the past. I trust that enough work will be generated through this web of relationships that my days of checking online job sites are just about over—although, just this past week I secured a job by responding to an online call for an editor.

The companies with which I now work are varied. The long-standing relationship I mentioned above is with a non-profit in Arizona, an organization that runs treatment facilities in several states. Some of them are in California prisons. The various projects they've handed me have been consistently fascinating and rewarding.

Another company I've worked for is run by a licensed Doctor of Optometry who also has a background in production and has established a company that delivers industrial videos to the eye care industry as well as a few other select industries. Very specialized work, but generally very well done. Their output is primarily educational or industrial, sometimes on DVD but, increasingly, on the web. Currently I've been working with them on developing a series of training videos for optometrists that can be accessed via the Internet, and in several different languages.

A few years back I edited a feature film starring Minnie Driver. The job came to me through the director, an agency colleague. That led me to work on a couple of documentaries with an editor who had won an Oscar for cutting *Rocky*.

I worked for a few years with a company in Ojai that booked touring musical acts. There I again ran the post-production department and designed and edited on computer. Actually cutting on videotape (linear editing) is pretty much a thing of the past these days. Once that was how it was done, with massive decks synchronized to each other and a single controller telling each machine what to play or record. But nowadays it's virtually all done on computer. Most of the TV spots produced in the last few years at this Ojai agency were sent to stations digitally from our small edit bay.

That job led me to relationships with artists like Eric Burdon (of *House of the Rising Sun* fame), Don Wilson of The Ventures, and the band Foghat. Working in Ojai led me to the source of most of my current work, a production company that posts several cable TV series and specials. This has been a wonderful relationship, as I can work from home at my own schedule, as long as the material gets delivered on time.

The only formal training I've had in nonlinear (computer-based) editing were a couple of weeklong classes at the start of my career. Beyond that, it has all been learn-on-the-job. The technical skills involved are complex, but relatively simple to master. In the dozen or so years since I started I have seen a tremendous expansion of access to the tools: powerful computers, editing and effects software, hard drives for storage, cameras, systems to capture the footage, hardware for managing and displaying footage, finishing tools such as DVD or Blu-ray authoring, and even Internet distribution via sites like YouTube or Vimeo.

When I started this career, access to an Avid was a highly prized commodity. The systems were expensive and the opportunity to actually edit something was very valuable. A working Avid system used to cost up to $100,000 but one can now set up an Apple-based professional-capable system for under $5,000. I now have my own (limited) Avid and a more fully functional Final Cut Pro system, on which I cut TV series and documentaries and the occasional feature film.

So as the tools have gotten cheaper and more common, so have editors who know which buttons to push because they've been to the same classes I went to fourteen years ago or because they've graduated from film school.

But I didn't feel like I knew how to edit—really knew how to edit—until just three or four years ago. Assembling footage into something flashy or lyrical-looking with speed changes, eye-catching transitions or smash cuts, that's not difficult to achieve. What takes time and experience to develop is the sense of storytelling, an understanding of the rhythm that a certain piece demands, the ability to completely hide the editing so the story appears to be seamlessly telling itself. It still requires the same storytelling instincts that any kind of literary narrative demands. It takes patience, openness and an eye for the fortuitous accident that can unlock a tricky story problem, but most of all I think it requires an ability to keep the long view in mind while wrestling with the immediate.

*Bruce's email is brucenovotny@verizon.net. He lives in Oxnard, California.*

I met Nancy Barnes when we were both exhibiting our books and promoting our editing services at the Central Coast Book & Author Festival in San Luis Obispo, California. Meeting another freelance editor is like meeting an old friend with whom you have a lot in common. Nancy is particularly personable and we decided to keep in touch. At the time (in September 2011) I didn't think about asking her to tell her story for this book but a few days after I returned home I realized that it would be a valuable addition to my book so I called her. She was very busy, working on a tight deadline but said she would get back to me as soon as possible. Only a couple of weeks later she emailed me her story. Here is what she wrote:

## Nancy Barnes's Story

When people talk about editing, too often it is described as a technical skill, as just a cold-blooded analysis of text. To me, editing is inextricably bound up in reading and writing. I hear the voice of the writer attempting to speak to me and I imagine all the possible ways those ideas could have been said and written down. Editing is actually very creative and fun, once you get beyond thinking there is just one correct way of doing it.

I've been a voracious reader since I was a child, and editing followed naturally. In fact, the first "long document" editing I can remember doing was at age fourteen, when I edited my mother's master's thesis. (She had a terrible tendency to run-on sentences.) Although I didn't foresee a career in editing, I was an English major in college, and inevitably my friends and coworkers in my various jobs asked me to edit their papers, their departmental reports, their marketing materials, their novels, etc. I became more skilled by puzzling through and solving the real problems each work presented.

My first freelance venture was as a business writer. Because I had been an English teacher, it was easy to pick up work developing and editing curriculum and instructional materials, and this rather dry academic material was my bread and butter until I accepted a part-time job in marketing and public relations. The publications I wrote and edited there had to be more readable, more visual, and more attractive to the reader than the technical and academic stuff, and this experience greatly improved my style as a writer and an editor.

I decided to focus on editing books when I became interested in family history and memoirs. This genre has lots of interesting possibilities, in terms of nonfiction narrative and design. My business, Stories To Tell Books, provides editing, book design, and self publishing services. This is a fairly specialized field, so I wrote a book, *Stories to Tell, An Easy Guide to Self Publishing Family History Books and Memoirs,* to educate authors about the process. One project has led to another, and people now hire me to work on all sorts of interesting book projects, fiction and nonfiction, private and commercial.

Unlike many editors, I like to work with first-time authors, and I shepherd many of my author's books all the way through the process. Authors who only need revisions to a more finished work are certainly easier to work with. They have already done some self editing, so they often know what they need and take instructions well from an editor.

Although anyone can write a book (or so they believe) design skills take years to learn. My authors need someone to format their finished draft into a publishable book, and there I am, positioned to accept that job. It took me years to master Photoshop to prepare images, Illustrator for cover design, and InDesign to lay out the book's interior. These technical skills are invaluable, as a source of income and also because I can show clients beautiful examples of my work. I don't recommend that every editor get into design, but being competent with computers and software is crucial in this business; so train yourself, constantly.

I have tried all sorts of pricing schemes in my work, and I still do. Generally, clients are confused and even suspicious, as they do not shop for these services often and it's tough to comparison shop for editing services. They understand an hourly rate most easily. I charge a lower-end hourly rate for some services, such as research, copy editing, and book design, which reassures prospects that my rates are affordable and competitive. I charge a higher rate for content editing, as it requires more skill. I use the standard 250-word-per-page count to estimate the number of pages of the manuscript, and depending on how much work it appears to need, I can guesstimate how many hours it will take to edit and/or design.

I often go through an informal negotiation with the client so that I can get a sense of what their budget is. I often offer two alternatives: the less expensive lesser service, or the more expensive higher quality service, so they feel they have choices. I sometimes offer all-in-one package pricing with a percentage discount, which appeals to the bargain hunters. I also offer monthly payment plans for big-ticket clients and for people on a tight budget, as this makes it possible for them to buy.

So far, I have had very positive relationships with my clients, and there are several dynamics that make that happen. My pricing is fair; and this leads to lots and lots of business, and those smaller profit margins really do add up. Second, I try to do one nice thing for each client in the course of our relationship, even if it is only sending a link to an article or book they might enjoy. That personal thoughtfulness creates a good reciprocal vibe, and clients often do nice things for me, right out of the blue! Some of my clients have become good, true friends, and this is one of the many joys of being self-employed.

Freelance editors, like other self-employed people, have to wear too many hats. I found the marketing and selling part of the business hardest. It must be done, one way or the other, and the sooner you get money coming in, the better. So if you can't sell successfully, hire a marketer, a web designer, a PR person, and spend whatever it takes to get the customers coming in.

I've seen a lot of beginning freelancers fail because the earnings were too slim in that first year. Of course, the safest way to start is to subcontract from someone who has too much work, or to have a day job in the field, so that you don't need a full-revenue freelance business at first.

There are other aspects of doing business, too: the communications, the bookkeeping, ordering the office supplies, the learning curve of the ever-changing technology, all of which will demand your attention and leach precious time away from your core money-making work. So how do you manage your workflow and run a successful editing business? It has to be your hobby. In the end, you have to really want to spend your time reading and writing, crouched in front of a computer screen for hours each day and/or night. I make my own hours, and I work a lot of hours. There's no getting around it. Fortunately, if you love to read and write, if it's something you already do for free as a hobby anyway, then all those other supporting chores you have to do to make it pay are worth the effort.

Freelancing isn't the easiest way to get paid to read and write. There are times I wish I had an employer to "take care of things" for me. You know, like healthcare, and paid vacation. Right . . . good luck finding that. So then I look around my home office, and yes there is a stack of work to be done, but it's mine, all mine. I play with my cat for a while, wander out to check what's in the fridge, and get back to work. So be it.

Nancy Barnes, www.StoriesToTellBooks.com
Stories To Tell Books
(888) 577-9342 (toll free)
www.StoriesToTellBooks.com
info@StoriesToTellBooks.com

As I was researching organizations, I came across Editorial Freelancers Association (EFA). It bills itself as "The professional resource for editorial specialists and those who hire them." I have described this organization in greater detail in another chapter. EFA's members have their bios on the website and as I was reading some of them I discovered Eileen Kramer's experience was just what I was looking for to include in this book. The following is an interview I had with her.

## Eileen Kramer's Story

**ME: How did you get started as a freelance editor?**

**EK:** I was working in the Statistics Department at Harvard University, using a computer program to typeset technical (math-heavy) articles and books written by the faculty. One of the post-docs asked if he could hire me as a freelancer to typeset his journal articles. This was Dr. Emery Brown, an anesthesiologist, who has become a world-famous expert on sleep science. Other graduate students and post-docs hired me for various projects as well; thus, my freelance career was launched.

**ME: Did you pursue this work or did it "find you"?**

**EK:** Well, it found me because I was open to the possibility, and because I was doing good work already in my day job.

**ME: In what field(s) and what kinds of documents do you edit?**

**EK:** This has changed over the years, and I expect will continue to change. I have an undergrad degree in biology and then took programming classes when I worked at Harvard, so my freelance editing has reflected my career changes and professional development. I began working mostly on math and statistics documents.

Then, in the 1990s, I had a full-time editing job at O'Reilly & Associates, which led to my involvement with the web. While at O'Reilly, I worked on the first graphical website news magazine in the world, called Global Network Navigator (later sold to

AOL). My work at O'Reilly and subsequent web development jobs changed my freelance editing to a new genre: computer science, information technology, and Internet applications.

I spent ten years as director of web development for a financial services company, Shareholder.com, which was bought by The Nasdaq in 2007. I got some money when Shareholder.com was acquired, and decided to go to graduate school and become an English teacher.

In 2008, I got my master's degree from the School for International Training (www.sit.edu), and since then have been teaching academic English to international students at Boston University. My freelance editing has subsequently included more and more textbooks.

Throughout the years and independent of the career changes, I have worked as a proofreader for MIT Press on three journals: *Neural Computation, Computer Music Journal,* and *The Review of Economics and Statistics.* Although the hourly rate has barely increased, I remain one of the Press's loyal freelancers. Why? They have high standards, excellent production managers, and interesting content.

**ME: What kind of expertise is required of an editor in your field?**

**EK:** While we tell prospective editors that they should be able to edit anything as long as they are well versed in grammar and usage, the truth is that most publishers want to hire freelancers who have some experience in the content field. For example, my biology degree indicates some familiarity with all sciences and math; therefore, I am more likely to be hired to edit a chemistry textbook than an excellent editor with thirty years' experience working on biographies.

Other requirements are comfort with technology and file management. When I teach copyediting, I tell my students that they must learn to use MS Word's Tools Tracker in order to be competitive. Being able to navigate the *Chicago Manual* and editing to APA (American Psychological Association) standards is another expectation.

**ME: Do you work directly with the author?**

**EK:** I have worked directly with authors several times, but usually with publishers or production houses. The biggest drawback to working directly with authors is their (understandable) lack of expertise in the editorial process. Regarding hard-copy edits, they rarely know the standard symbols so it takes much longer to make comprehensible edits. They may also be too close to the work to want an editor, but they know they need one. I prefer to work with an author's representative.

**ME: Do you have any words of wisdom for those who are thinking of pursuing a career as a freelance editor?**

**EK:** Oh good, I was hoping you'd ask.

1.  Why do you want to be a freelance editor? Many people are under the impression that freelance editing means you get to stay home in your pj's, calmly reading interesting manuscripts, and getting dressed only to take your checks to the bank. Does this scenario happen? Yes, sometimes it really is this peaceful and easy. But don't count on it. Most freelance editing jobs involve tough deadlines, multiple authors with inconsistent writing styles, and content that you may or may not find intriguing.

2.  Don't quit your day job. If you are financially comfortable and want to try something new, then go ahead and become a freelance editor. However, if you are living paycheck to paycheck and just want to strike out on your own, consider the financial consequences very carefully. You will not have health insurance unless your spouse/partner can provide it, and your income will become unpredictable. Try freelancing first as a supplement to

your income. Find out if your skills are marketable. Test the waters before diving in headfirst.

3. Network. Network. Network. Freelancers do not have to be recluses; you need colleagues. We are fortunate to have a national organization of freelance publishing professionals, the Editorial Freelancers Association (www.the-efa.org). There are local/regional chapters in many states, and the chapter meetings are a prime opportunity for networking with other freelancers. If you are thinking of becoming a freelancer, go to one of the chapter meetings and talk to people. Ask where they find work, how they got started, and what advice they have for you.

4. Use the contacts you already have. The best way to get started as a freelancer is to take your contacts with you on this journey. Tell the relevant people in your life that you are available for freelance work. Ask them to tell all of their business contacts about you too. Market your newly invented freelance self.

*Eileen F. Kramer has an undergraduate degree in biology and she has been a freelance copyeditor of technical journals and science/math textbooks for many years. Contact her at Kramer@tiac.net.*

## HOW YOU CAN GET STARTED

Once you have a goal in mind, what might otherwise be idle conversation can turn into important information that can lead you to your first client. When you feel that you are ready to launch your own freelance editing career, start making contacts. Here are a few ideas of what you might want to do.

• Get to know people in your field. Go to conventions, expos, and grand openings and be sure to talk to as many people as you can. Let them know about your interest in and qualifications for editing text.

- Ask questions. Find out if companies use freelance writers and editors. Even if they have in-house writers, they still may want to hire freelance editors who are familiar with their services or products. It could be more cost-effective for companies to pay per project instead of having editors on their staff.

- Join an editing organization or company that can get you assignments. There are several such groups listed on the Internet and they include information on how to join and what the dues or membership fees are.

- Join writer's groups and book clubs if your interest is in editing books. Let the writers and book lovers who are thinking about writing a book know that you are an editor.

- Attend events where writers in your specialty gather. For instance, if your specialty is memoir and autobiography, a genealogy group might be interested in your services.

- Discuss your freelance editing career with friends and acquaintances. Let them know you are looking for clients. They may know of a company or individual who is looking for an editor.

- Opportunities are everywhere. Keep your antenna up at all times. You never know where your clients might come from.

# ❦3❧

## *Careers in Editing*

What kind of editing do you have training and experience in? Do you want to be a specialist or a generalist? As no one person can edit all kinds of documents, specializing may make the most sense. Editing a book is different from editing a magazine or newspaper article. For instance, in books we use italics to indicate the title of a book, magazine, movie, stage play, TV series, newspaper, magazine, and so forth. But in the *New Yorker* magazine, they enclose those titles in quotation marks. They do use italics but usually it is only for foreign language words and phrases. One style does not fit all.

Editing a textbook is different from editing a novel or nonfiction book. It requires a different mindset. Textbooks are written in a formal style. Novels can be very informal. And some books break a number of rules and it is okay for that particular book if the publisher of it says it is okay. For example, in Frank McCourt's memoir *'Tis,* there are no quotation marks in the entire book and he writes a lot of dialog. Some of his sentences ramble on for 300 or 400 words, separated only by an occasional comma. It made me breathless just reading it silently to myself. McCourt was a high school teacher. It isn't as though he didn't know how to punctuate. His novel was published by Scribner, a major publishing house. Apparently, they figured this was McCourt's style and they didn't want to mess with it. Editors should stick to the rules—usually—however they should also be flexible and bend to the author's or publisher's will when called upon to do so.

Being a good editor of memoirs and biographies does not mean that you can edit all kinds of books and all types of writing. In some cases, you will need to have some experience and knowledge in the subject and an understanding of the styles used. Theses, dissertations, medical, technical, and scientific writing all have their own styles. Do you prefer formal styles or popular styles of writing? Do you want to work with companies and organizations or with individuals? What do you expect from your new freelance business? These are questions you need to consider before you begin. I have found that, generally, what you do best is what you enjoy the most, and vice versa.

## DETERMINING THE KIND OF EDITING YOU WILL DO

The websites of editing organizations can give you additional information on various fields of editing. Many of them also help you promote your services and provide prospective clients with information about you.

In all forms of editing the most time consuming and expensive problems to correct are the organization of the material. This is the case whether the document is a doctoral dissertation, a grant proposal, a magazine article, a how-to book, or a novel.

The following are a few of the kinds of documents you might wish to specialize in.

### Doctoral Dissertations

To illustrate the importance of learning the standards and styles of specific kinds of documents, I give as an example the doctoral dissertation. This is a formal document that requires a strict adherence to professional standards and styles. An editor must be familiar with the requirements of a dissertation and have on hand the reference book that describes the American Psychological Association (APA) editorial style. It covers styles of punctuation, spelling, capitalization, italics, abbreviations, headings, quotations, and numbers, to name only a few. The stylebook is the *Publication Manual of the American Psychological Association.* Many journals in psychology, the behavioral sciences, nursing, and personnel administration also use the *APA Publication Manual* as their style guide.

The stylebook for dissertations is different from other stylebooks, such as those for magazines, journals, and books. This is where specialization comes in handy. It is not easy to switch to APA styles if one has been editing books for the general reader. As I do both, I always get the APA stylebook out and reacquaint myself with the APA style before I begin editing a dissertation. For instance, the style for a dissertation bibliography is different from that of a book bibliography. Every time I've had to reformat that section for a client I have wondered why that can't be standardized for all kinds of writing. But that's the way it is and it isn't likely to change any time soon.

Like most writing, structuring the manuscript is the most difficult aspect of writing a dissertation. The writer must organize the evidence and discussions that support the thesis into a logical and articulate form. The editor must determine whether it has satisfied all the rules of formal grammar. It can't contain contractions, slang, colloquialisms, undefined jargon, or slurs. It must convey the meaning intended precisely.

## Magazine Articles

When working with manuscripts for books, the editor doesn't have to be too concerned about whether the writing is concise. The author has the luxury of expanding on the subject. Most trade books have about 30,000 to 80,000 words. The same is not true for magazine articles. Articles for consumer magazines must cover the material in a limited number of words ranging from around 250 to 4,000 words. Magazine editors are looking for short feature articles that cover a specific subject. They want crisp writing.

When you have a client who wants you to edit his article, your first consideration should be to determine whether the author has done his homework and researched the guidelines for submitting articles—and they vary from publication to publication. He must know what types of articles the magazine is looking for. He should have an idea of the length of the article he should submit. If the author does not have experience in writing articles, you must put on a different hat—that of a consultant. If he hasn't targeted his article for a particular type of magazine and does not know the guidelines for it, editing his article isn't going to be very helpful to him. You can either explain to him how to find that information or offer to do it for him. *Writer's Market* (Writer's Digest Books) has this information. Be sure to get the most recent edition.

Magazine editors look for good informational writing that is aimed at their audience. Nonfiction editors want short features that cover a particular subject. If the writer is not an expert in the subject, she must make herself one through research to be qualified to write on the subject. The writer should always query before sending her article. The query should not be emailed or faxed unless the listing indicates it is acceptable.

Fiction editors usually want to see the complete manuscript. As this is a highly competitive market, they may not respond to submissions unless they are interested in publishing it. For more information on fiction markets, see *Novel & Short Story Writer's Market* (also published by Writer's Digest Books).

In either case, it is important to do a thorough job of researching the guidelines for each magazine the author will be submitting his article to. In addition to that, the writer should check the magazine's website, read several issues of the magazine, and if possible talk to an editor on the phone.

Once the writer has done the above research and is ready to have his article edited, you can begin. Conciseness is a major consideration. A lot of information has to be condensed into a few words without making the writing seem choppy and hurried. All of the other principles that apply to book editing also apply to article editing. The major difference is the length of the manuscript.

## Screenwriting

As a freelance editor you are not likely to be editing scripts for an established film or television studio or production company. They are edited in-house in almost all cases. You might be called upon to edit a spec script by an individual, though. And to do that you have to understand the major differences between a script and a book. For the writer, the formatting is paramount because there are many different acceptable formats for various kinds of scripts. An editor isn't usually expected to know all of the different formats but she should alert the writer that they exist and suggest that he get copies of various scripts to study them.

As an editor, you should understand the basic script style so that you can guide the scriptwriter. For example, in scripts there are rarely long conversations. The dialog should be written in short sentences, and the characters should be realistic. Spec scripts should not contain visual cues and camera directions. That should be left to the director and producer.

Scripts are harder than you might think to write and to edit. A screenplay is a story told with pictures and it is not at all like writing a book. Scripts are harder to sell than book manuscripts. According to most experts in the field, if a writer has a really good idea and great story, he should first write it as a book. If the book sells well it won't be so hard to interest a producer in adapting it for the screen. The author may even have a shot at writing the script or at least co-writing it with an experienced screenwriter. Although this is not your concern as an editor, it is worthwhile advice to give to a prospective writer/client.

I saw firsthand how difficult it is for a novice to write a successful script and how futile it could be to edit a poorly written script. Some years ago I was a script reader for an independent film and television production company located at Universal Studios. As a company that had produced successful films and television series in the past, they had been given an office on the Universal lot to use while they searched for their next production. There was no staff or crew because the company wasn't currently in production. There were only three of us: the producer, the director (who rarely came into the office) and me. I doubled as assistant to the producer and script reader but I spent most of my time reading spec scripts.

After he hired me, the producer, who was looking for a new property to produce, accepted all submissions. I started out by reading each script in its entirety, then writing up a critique of it to give to the producer along with the script, which he could look at himself to make the decision. After awhile, when he realized that my summations and opinions were consistent with his own, he told me not to write critiques on hopelessly horrible scripts because he didn't want to waste his time, or mine, on such material. I was relieved because we must have received about a dozen submissions a day and the scripts were piling up on a table in the corner of the office. And I could only read and write a critique on two or three a day. To be fair to the scriptwriter, I paperclipped a note with the date each script arrived so that I could read them in the order in which they were submitted.

After a few weeks I stopped reading entire scripts, too, because I realized that by reading only about ten or so pages I could tell whether the script had any merit at all. By not reading each bad script to the bitter end, I could get to more scripts. There were many scripts where all I had to do was read the first page to tell that it was from a writer who had no command of the English language. There were spelling, grammatical, and punctuation errors screaming out at me. At first I thought, well, I'll read a few more pages to see if he at least has an interesting story here and if so, maybe a good editor can bring it out. But I soon gave up on that fantasy. If a writer is sloppy about the craft of writing, he will be sloppy about crafting a story. To tell a story well it helps to know the basic principles of writing. If the writing is bad it is hard to get to the meat of the story.

There were other signs that the writer didn't do her homework before writing and handing in her spec script. The most obvious sign of an amateur is a script that is not formatted properly. This requires a certain amount of research into the standard format for each kind of script. A script for a stage play is formatted one way, for a TV series it is formatted another way, and a script for a feature-length film is formatted still another way. The wrong format instantly tells the experienced script reader that the writer hasn't even taken the time to find out what the requirements are.

There is even a font that is preferred for each kind of script and the writer should find out what it is for the type of script he is writing. Although the standard for most book manuscripts is Times Roman, 12 point, there is not just one standard for all scripts. Years ago the most commonly used font was Courier, which looks a lot like a standard typewriter font. But I'm sure that has changed too.

During the time I worked there I read at least half a dozen a day. When I came across one that I thought had possibilities, I would read the entire script and write my critique of it for the producer. In the space of a year I found only four or five scripts that the producer, director, and I all agreed had promise.

Very often a script written by an established screenwriter was sent directly to the producer by the writer's agent and I never saw it. For the most part the scripts I read were by novice writers and they were not submitted by agents. I was pleased to know that the producers I worked for wanted to give unknown writers a chance. Who knows where the next great story—and screenplay—will come from?

If you find yourself being asked to edit a screenplay, I suggest you get Syd Field's excellent book, *Screenplay: The Foundations of Screenwriting; A Step-by-Step Guide from Concept to Finished Script*. This book should help you in your job of editing a screenplay. And, perhaps more importantly, it is a book that you can advise your client to get and study as he is writing.

## Books

My specialty is editing trade books. Trade books are defined as those that have been published through commercial publishers and are marketed to the public. These can be from established book publishers as well as self-publishers.

The best guide for deciding the kinds of books you will enjoy editing will be your own reading preferences. What kind of book do you read for pleasure and/or information? Do you lean toward fiction such as historical novels, adventure, romance, and mysteries? Or do you tend to read mostly nonfiction. If your interest is mainly in nonfiction, you will likely be able to edit nonfiction books better than other kinds of material. To further specialize, you can choose specific categories of nonfiction, such as biography, memoir, how-to, or self-help. If you prefer to read novels, then fiction may be a better fit for you.

As a freelance editor rather than an editor who is on the staff of a book publishing company, you will most likely be working directly with an author who hires you and pays your fees herself. Oftentimes you won't be choosing the kind of book you will edit; you will probably be contacted by authors who have heard of you or met you at some kind of gathering for authors and publishers. And many of them will decide to self-publish, so that author/publisher will be your only boss. He is the only one you have to please. She is the one to whom you owe your best effort.

If you have been presented with a manuscript in a genre that you have no experience with, you will have to make the difficult decision of whether or not to take it on. For instance, even though you may not have edited a children's book before and rarely even looked at one, you may have an author ask you to edit the one she has written. If you have not had a client for a while and really need to make some money to pay your bills, you may be tempted to take the job. When you are just beginning it is best that you don't try to edit the kinds of books you are unfamiliar with. It is a disservice to the author because you lack the knowledge and experience to edit a book in that genre.

You need to know a great deal about the genre you are working with. Remember, when you are starting out, you are building your reputation. You'll want to do a good job with whatever book you are editing, not only because it is the right thing to do but because you are more likely to get a referral from that client. Eventually you may learn more about children's books and be able to edit them proficiently. But at the beginning of your career, stick with what you already know.

## Book Genres

There are two basic categories: fiction and nonfiction. The following is a general list of genres. It is a composite of several different lists. There are a number of subgenres as well.

## Fiction

Narrative literary works produced by the imagination and not necessarily based on fact. This category includes:

**Chapter Books.** Transitional books for ages 7 through 10 that help children move from early readers to full novels. Most chapter books deal with contemporary situations that are familiar to the readers, and are often humorous books.

**Fable.** Story that teaches a lesson or moral. Characters are usually animals who speak as humans.

**Fairy Tale.** Story about fairies or other magical creatures.

**Fantasy.** Fiction with characters or settings that could not exist in the real world.

**Folklore.** Stories, myths, and proverbs of a people as handed down by word of mouth.

**Graphic Novel.** A story in graphic form, long comic strip, or heavily illustrated story.

**Historical Fiction.** A story with fictional characters and events in a historical setting.

**Horror.** Stories that evoke a feeling of dread in both the characters and the reader.

**Humor.** Fiction meant to be funny and entertaining; can be contained in all genres.

**Mystery.** A story dealing with solving a crime and usually the unraveling of secrets.

**Mythology.** Stories that reveal human behavior and natural phenomena through symbolism; often pertaining to the actions of gods.

**Picture books.** This is a book with illustrations that play a significant role in telling the story. Traditionally, they are 32-page books for ages 4 through 8.

**Poetry.** Verse and rhythmic writing with imagery that creates emotional responses.

**Realistic Fiction.** True-to-life stories.

**Science Fiction.** Stories based on actual, imagined, or potential science.

**Short Stories.** Brief fiction, usually in a collection.

**Young adult novels, also called teen novels.** Most are stories involving contemporary problems, including drugs, sex, and peer pressure. They are generally read by children age 12 through 18.

There is an almost endless list of genres, depending on where your research leads you. Some blur the line between fiction and nonfiction. Among them are the following:

**Autobiographical Novel.** This has also been called **Fictional Autobiography**. For a novel to be considered autobiographical by most standards, there must be a protagonist modeled after the author and a central plot that mirrors events in his or her life. To be considered fiction, much of the story must be from the imagination of the author. Many autobiographies do not always portray real people and adhere to true events and the author of an autobiographical novel is free to write whatever she pleases without worrying about being sued. Well, maybe. Some autobiographical novelists have described a character in a way that the character becomes recognizable as an actual person to the reader. If the author portrays that character in a very unfavorable light, he may be subject to a defamation of character lawsuit.

**Fictional Memoir.** The most notable novel I have seen with this definition was *Memoirs of a Geisha* by Arthur Golden, who writes it in first person in the voice of a geisha. He admits that he threw out all 800 pages of the manuscript he had written after he met a retired geisha and she told him her story. Much of the book is based on a real geisha and her actual experiences. However, the author also did a great deal of research on the history of the profession and the era in which the story was set.

**Creative Nonfiction, also known as Literary Nonfiction.** A branch of writing that employs the literary techniques usually associated with fiction or poetry to report on actual persons, places, or events. The genre is broad enough to include travel, nature, and science writing; biography, autobiography, memoir, the interview, and personal essay.

**Nonfiction Novel.** To quote Encyclopedia Britannica, a nonfiction novel is a "story of actual people and actual events told with the dramatic techniques of a novel." The American writer Truman Capote claimed to have invented this genre with his book *In Cold Blood* (1965). The book was about the brutal murder of a farm family in Kansas. It was a true story and Capote spent six years researching and interviewing neighbors and friends of the victims as well as the two murderers. He told the story from the characters' (actual people he interviewed) point of view and tried not to include his own comments or distort any of the facts.

There were actually earlier precedents for this type of journalistic novel, such as John Hersey's *Hiroshima* (1946), an account of the World War II atomic bombing of the Japanese city told through the histories of six survivors. Another was Norman Mailer's *The Executioner's Song* (1979). The book was about Gary Gilmore, who robbed and brutally murdered two men in 1976. Mailer focuses on the last nine months in the troubled existence of Gilmore, who, at the time Mailer wrote the book, was the first criminal executed in the United States in more than a decade.

## Nonfiction

Informational books that deal with actual, real-life subjects. The dictionary definition of nonfiction is "literary works other than fiction." The list is long and includes the following:

Art, Architecture, and Photography
Biography and Autobiography
Business and Economics
Computers and Technology
Cooking, Food, and Wine
Current Events
Education
Family and Relationships
Film, Video, and Theater
Foreign Language Study
Games
Health and Fitness
History
House and Home
Humor/Comedy
Jokes and Riddles
Law
Literary Criticism
Mathematics
Medical
Pets

Philosophy
Poetry
Political Science
Psychology
Reference
Sports and Recreation
Study Aids
Travel
True Crime

It would be impossible for anyone to know all there is to know about editing books in all genres. However, although you don't edit all books alike, most of the principles regarding punctuation, spelling, sentence structure, grammar, and usage are the same. You will most likely run across many things in the editing process that you have questions about.

Before you take your first job, get the most recent edition of *The Chicago Manual of Style* and become acquainted with it. There is a great deal of information in it. It will take some time to get used to the layout of the book and learn how and where to find the answers to your questions.

There are over a thousand pages in the 16th Edition, published in 2010. Some of the changes from previous editions include producing electronic publications, web-based content, and e-books. Always get the most up-to-date edition of the *Manual* so that you can keep current. Publishing has changed dramatically in this digital age and the most recent edition provides a wealth of new information and guidelines for electronic workflow and processes. There are new formats, new procedures, new sources, and new usages that define the publishing industry today. To quote the website for the 16th edition, "If you work with words—no matter what the delivery medium—this is the one reference you simply must have." You can buy it from the publisher, The University of Chicago Press, from a bookstore, or online.

After you start your editing career you may find that you can expand your areas of expertise. Sometimes this just happens without your even looking for it. After a few years of editing books I started editing doctoral dissertations as well. I did not seek out other kinds of written material to edit. I was happy to specialize in books and there is such a large variety of them that I could never become complacent or bored. There is always so much more to learn.

However, I became an editor of dissertations on the insistence of one of my clients, whose book I had edited. I explained to her that I had never edited dissertations—I had never even written any—but she believed I could do it, based on my editing of her book. As I was not all that confident that I could do a good job I decided that I had to educate myself on this type of work. I got several dissertations and read them and I bought the *Publication Manual of the American Psychological Association* to become familiar with the explicit style requirements of it before I began. Dissertations are not my favorite things to edit—I much prefer books—but because of that client's subsequent referrals it gave me another income stream. As a freelancer, that can help you avoid the inevitable slow times.

## ORGANIZATIONS FOR FREELANCE EDITORS

Anyone wishing to join an editing organization or a company that promotes and sells the services of an editor should research it as much as possible to be sure that it will serve their needs. Some might be very helpful to you as a freelance editor, both with useful information on how to break into the field, and in putting you in touch with prospective clients—or them in touch with you. But since you are required to pay a membership or registration fee and, in some cases, give them 50 percent of your commissions, you should investigate carefully to find out if they deliver what they promise—and what you need.

Among the businesses and organizations described below are those that specialize in book editing, medical and scientific editing, business editing, and those that do not specialize but cover all kinds of editing. The following organizations are among many you can find on the

Internet. I have chosen only a few to illustrate their specialties and criteria for membership.

### Editorial Freelancers Association (EFA); www.the-efa.org

A good source of information is the Editorial Freelancers Association. They call themselves "The professional resource for editorial specialists and those who hire them." This is a national not-for-profit organization—a 501(c)6—headquartered in New York City. Its members live and work in forty-five of the United States and in Canada, England, France, Ireland, Israel, and Japan. There are regional chapters outside New York City and members can also network with each other on the email discussion list which is moderated.

Its members benefit from EFA's email discussion list, Job List service, newsletter, publications, and online education courses. Any full-time or part-time freelancer may join. If you subscribe to the Job List service you will receive email notification of job opportunities. According to the EFA's website, companies, agencies, and individuals searching for help use EFA's free job-posting service which puts them in touch with more than 1,000 experienced freelancers nationwide. The following is a list of its members' specialties:

Advertising–public relations
Arts–culture
Business–financial
Children–young adult
Computer technology
Cookbooks
Corporate communications
Ecology–environment
Education
Fiction
History
Humor

Legal
Politics
Psychology
Reference
Religion-spiritual
Scholarly-textbooks
Science
Technical
Training manuals
Women's studies

The membership includes:

abstractors
copyeditors
designers
desktop publishing experts
editors
indexers
manuscript evaluators
picture researchers
project managers
proofreaders
researchers
textbook development editors
translators
writers

## Northwest Independent Editors Guild; (www.edsguild.org)

Another such organization is the Northwest Independent Editors Guild, an alliance of professional editors in Alaska, Idaho, Oregon, and Washington. It is a networking group for freelance editors, not an employment or placement agency. They do not certify their members and are not involved in the client-editor relationship. They do, however, let clients post their project or job on the Guild's job board. Clients then search the membership directory and choose from their list of editors.

## Society of American Business Editors and Writers (SABEW); www.sabew.org

Membership is restricted to those whose occupations involve writing, reporting, editing or overseeing business, financial, or economic news for newspapers, magazines, newsletters, journals, books, press or syndicated services, radio or television, online publications, or other media approved by the SABEW board of governors. Teachers and students of business journalism or business media subjects at recognized colleges, universities, or other organizations approved by the Society's board may also qualify for membership. Members have full access to the SABEW website, including the searchable database. Individual memberships are $50 each. Students pay only $10.

## Book Editing Associates; www.book-editing.com

This is a quote from their website: "The core focus of this network is talent, ethics, and the proper writer–editor match." This is a network of freelance editors/independent contractors, so the agreement/arrangement is between the client and the writer/editor, not the network as a whole or the network coordinator. On their website they state that they need *fiction* specialists (mainstream and genre) who can perform all of the following services: developmental editing, copyediting/line editing, proofreading, and fact checking. Preference will be given to applicants who intend to commit long-term, submit a bio written in third person, and provide verifiable feedback/references from clients (published writers). For more information on joining, go to their website.

## EditAvenue.com; www.editavenue.com

Their subtitle is The Online Editing Service Marketplace. This is an online platform for document editing commerce. The system manages a group of consultants who quasi-independently perform editing services. All trade and communications between editors and clients are performed and regulated within the system. Editors pay a $35 editor registration fee to become members and 50 percent of their commissions to EditAvenue.com.

### Papercheck; www.papercheck.com/business

Papercheck is a business editing service for websites, emails, memos, business proposals, grants, sales contracts, brochures, and other formal business documents. Papercheck provides grammar editing, which includes the correction of punctuation, verb tense, spelling, and sentence structure.

The following are several websites advertising medical and scientific editing services. Many of them also carry employment opportunity sections. Some of them break down their services into three standard levels: basic, advanced, and professional.

**Basic** includes proofreading and some basic editorial services that cover correcting spelling, grammar, punctuation, and consistency in formatting the document. They estimate that basic service will require an hour to edit about five pages.

**Advanced** covers all the basic services plus editing for clarity, style, and content. It includes eliminating jargon (a very real concern in medical and scientific documents), and some rewriting to improve the flow. At this level about four pages can be edited in an hour.

**Professional** level covers all of the above as well as content editing of complex material. It also includes reorganizing the material and correcting style inconsistencies. It may include significant rewriting for clarity. About two to three pages can be edited in an hour at this level.

They also provide an estimation of the time required at each level. At higher levels of editing, fewer pages can be edited.

Medical and scientific editing includes the following types of documents:

Abstracts
Books

Brochures and Reports
Dissertations and Theses
Editorials
Galley Proofs
Grant Proposals and Revisions
Letters
Manuscripts
Philosophy Statements
Reviews
Reviewer Responses
Slide and Poster Presentations
Technical Writing

## American Medical Writers Association (AMWA); www.amwa.org

If you plan to go into the medical field of editing, AMWA is the leading professional organization for writers, editors, and other communicators of medical information. There are networking opportunities through an annual conference and job services, including Jobs Online and a Freelance Directory. They publish the *AMWA Journal*, an indexed, peer-reviewed publication.

## Council of Science Editors (CSE); www.councilscienceeditors.org

This is specifically for science editors. It is a community of editorial professionals dedicated to the responsible and effective communication of science. CSE's stated mission is "to serve editorial professionals in the sciences by creating a supportive network for career development, providing educational opportunities, and developing resources for identifying and implementing high-quality editorial practices." They also publish a stylebook titled *Scientific Style and Format: the CSE Manual for Authors, Editors, and Publishers.*

## BioScience Writers; www.biosciencewriters.com

BioScience Writers describes itself as "a group of research scientists with expertise in scientific grant development, manuscript preparation, and report editing." Their staff frequently reviews NIH grant proposals and journal submissions to keep abreast of the standards and expectations of reviewers. They state that their editors are "accustomed to helping non-native English speakers perfect their scientific texts." The rates charged by scientific and medical editors are among the highest. However, their editors almost always have advanced degrees and their editing is highly specialized. In checking out their website I found that all of the editors listed had either PhDs or MDs. They offer editing and proofreading services on many types of medical and scientific documents. Their services include creating tables and figures and embedding images to provide the most appealing presentation.

## The Medical Editor; www.themedicaleditor.com

The Medical Editor offers medical editing and rewriting services for medical and scientific manuscripts, book-length projects, grant applications, dissertations, theses, and other technical documents in biology, biomedicine, and biotechnology. They state that they edit in four key areas. These are:

(1) **Substantive medical editing** which includes rewriting sentences, deleting redundancies, restructuring paragraphs, removing jargon, checking usage, and making sure that the manuscript clearly and effectively presents its information.

(2) **Medical copyediting and proofreading** to meet stylistic requirements of the American Medical Association. This includes editing for sense, style, consistency, preferred usage, grammar, spelling, punctuation, and capitalization.

(3) **Formatting** references, text, tables, figures, and legends so that they conform to the journal's instruction to authors or to the

Uniform Requirements for Manuscripts Submitted to Biomedical Journals.

(4) **Reference accuracy.** Verifying the accuracy of the reference section at the National Library of Medicine.

There are even organizations for freelancers in general. And these can be very helpful to the independent contractor, consultant, and self-employed person who can be left out of the traditional social safety net, such as access to affordable insurance, unemployment insurance, and retirement plans. Independent workers make up 30 percent of the nation's workforce—and that percentage is rising. The following is one organization that sponsors nationwide seminars, workshops, and events.

### Freelancers Union, http://freelancersunion.org

Freelancers Union represents independent workers as a group. They help freelancers get access to dental, life, and disability insurance nationwide. It is a nonprofit advocacy organization with a 501(c)4 status that promotes fairness for consultants, independent contractors, temps, part-timers, contingent employees, and the self-employed. It is an organization where freelancers can help each other through networking, collaboration, and sharing knowledge. According to the Freelancers Union, "The problem is simply that there hasn't been a movement to represent the needs of independent workers. Freelancers Union is that movement."

The above listings are merely a few examples of the many companies and organizations that work with editors, writers, and other freelancers. I can't endorse any of them because I don't know enough about them to make any recommendations. I'd suggest you get more information before you become involved with them.

# 4

## *Marketing Your Services*

No matter how good you are at what you do, if no one knows about you it will be hard—no, impossible—to make a living as a freelance editor. You must promote and market your services. At first I made a few mistakes in trying to get clients. I advertised in the local newspaper and got quite a few calls, but mostly from wannabe writers, not serious writers. Many of them wanted me to edit the first chapter of their book for free and if they liked what I did they might hire me to edit the rest of it. Some stated that they were auditioning several editors and would choose the one they liked best after seeing how they all edited several pages of their manuscript. I can't imagine spending even an hour editing for someone who was only "auditioning" me along with several other editors without paying me for my time.

Many prospective clients have only a fuzzy idea of what an editor actually does or how much the editing would cost. Some expected to pay in the neighborhood of ten dollars an hour or a hundred dollars for a 200-page manuscript. As I saw that as starvation wages, I politely turned them down. No one can edit hurriedly and edit well. It's one or the other.

In the long run, most of my clients came to me through referrals from other clients, from people who had attended my seminars and workshops, from those who had read about me in local newspapers or on the Internet or those who read my book *Author's Toolkit*. As most of them already had an idea of my rates, there wasn't a problem with sticker shock.

To get the word out that I was a book editor (my specialty) I started finding venues where I could speak, such as writers club meetings, writers conferences, book festivals, and other places where writers gather.

## DONATING TIME AND EXPERTISE TO NONPROFITS

Volunteering is another one of those win–win activities. While you are donating your services you are networking with people who could use your expertise as an editor. You could offer to write and/or edit their monthly newsletter, help organize their meetings, or edit their grant proposals. Once they get to know you and love you, you can offer to conduct a seminar or speak to their group about writing, which leads to the next marketing idea.

## SPEAKING AND CONDUCTING WORKSHOPS

If you are interested in becoming a freelance editor you probably have some experience in writing and/or teaching. Possibly you have been an editor on the staff of a company that needed your expertise. You are probably very knowledgeable about grammar, sentence structure, and composition. Write a list of all the things you know about editing and writing. Make notes of errors you have found in newspaper and magazine articles, books, advertising copy, etc. and think about the information you could impart to a group of less knowledgeable people.

Nearly everybody I've spoken to says they want to write a book. And nearly everybody could write a book. We all have something to say, stories to tell, information to impart. But most people can't write it in a professional way. Some of the most famous authors have their editor to thank for getting their book ready to be published. In many cases, it has been the editor who made all the difference between merely an interesting book and an outstanding one.

You could share your knowledge with writers and at the same time promote your services through public speaking. It would be nice to be paid for your educational presentations but, even if you aren't, it is beneficial to you because writers will learn about you and what you do. Consider contacting a nonprofit organization, a writers club, or a literary organization and letting them know you are available to speak to their group. Put together a few subjects you can cover and an outline of what you will say. Also write a brief bio about yourself covering your experience and education.

If you have never presented a seminar or taught a workshop, that's okay. You have to start sometime if you want to promote your services. Why not now?

## NETWORKING

Joining and taking part in organizations for writers is a great way to promote your services. Get familiar with both local and national organizations for writers and editors. As your clients will be writers it's a good idea to go to places and events where writers congregate. Attend writer organizations' meetings, especially the local ones because that is where you will meet the people who may need your services. If possible, get on their board of directors. Offer to give educational presentations at their meetings. As an editor you have a lot of valuable information to give to writers, not only about editing their own works but about the presentation of their manuscripts.

If there aren't any organizations for writers in your area, start one yourself. When I first started out I couldn't figure out how to let writers know about my services. I couldn't afford to advertise at first and later, when I did, I attracted the wrong kind of client. I realized that for me, advertising wasn't going to work. I had to learn to promote my editing business but I didn't know much about promoting. I had never been in sales. I had worked in the production side of the television industry until I launched my freelance editing career. I didn't have a product to sell, I had a service to sell; something that you can't see, play, drive, or hold in your hand.

But to market my services I had to find and talk to the consumers who, in this case, were writers who needed to get their books polished and brought up to book publishing standards. There was, and still is, a writers club in a nearby city and their meetings were held in a location about 30 miles away. That group is the Ventura County Writers Club, a terrific organization for writers that was formed in 1932! They have monthly meetings that are open to the public. They also host a number of individual critique groups organized by genres (such as novels, children's books, memoirs, how-to books and so forth). The groups meet regularly at member's homes.

I have attended the Club's monthly meetings as often as I can. I have also spoken several times to their group, sharing some of my expertise on writing and editing books for publication, preparing book proposals, and seeking an agent and/or publisher. It is not only a pleasure for me but it lets writers know how I may be able to help them. However, the Writers Club (at that time) didn't address the business of writing. They were more about the art and craft of writing. I wanted to meet writers who were seriously interested in getting published or in learning how to publish their works themselves. I was looking for a group that drew not only writers but illustrators, cover designers, literary agents, and book publishers.

Since I couldn't find such a group I decided to start one myself and in 1996 I founded Small Publishers, Artists & Writers Network (SPAWN) which in the beginning was simply a networking group. Its stated purpose was "to promote the literary arts and to provide education, information, resources, and networking opportunities for artists, graphic designers, writers, and other creative individuals interested in the publishing process."

Once I had established an organization and rounded up some interested writers willing to volunteer their time, I planned our first meeting. I found an interesting location for the meeting in Old Town, Ventura. It was a large room in a historic building called The Livery, which had once been a stable where horses and vehicles were kept in the early 1900s. Then I phoned a well-known publisher whose offices were in North Hollywood and asked him if he would come and speak to our group. He was very gracious and asked me how many people would be attending the meeting. I said, "I don't know."

"How many usually attend?" he asked.

"This will be the first meeting, so I have no idea how many people will be there," I explained. There was a long pause on the other end of the line and I held my breath. Then I added, "And I would like to take you to dinner beforehand."

"That would be nice," he said. "I would also like to bring my senior editor, as she has a lot of valuable advice for writers, too."

I gulped, thinking of the expense, but quickly said, "Oh yes. I'd like to meet her too."

"Where will this meeting be held?"

"In a lovely old historic building in Ventura," I said.

"In Ventura? That's about an hour from the San Fernando Valley, isn't it?"

"Yes," I admitted. Again there was a pause.

Finally, he said, "Yes, we'll be there."

The publisher was Melvin Powers who owned the Wilshire Book Company. His company published hundreds of books, including *Psycho-Cybernetics: A New Technique for Using Your Subconscious Power,* which sold over three million copies. He certainly didn't need to drive nearly sixty miles to attend a meeting of who knows how many people put together by someone he had never heard of. He didn't need the promotion or the free dinner. But he accepted my invitation.

Having dipped into my savings to rent the meeting room and take Melvin and his editor wife out to dinner, I was worried about how the event would turn out. I wrote a news release and sent it to newspapers from Santa Barbara to Los Angeles, including several local (Ventura County) papers. In the news release I mentioned that the speaker was a very successful book publisher. I knew that writers would be interested in meeting a publisher in person and have the opportunity to ask him questions. And, who knows? He might even agree to look at their book manuscript with an eye toward publishing it. How often does a writer have that opportunity? The news release also stated that a $5 donation was requested.

On the evening of the meeting, I took Melvin and his senior editor, who is also his wife, to a nice restaurant in another historic building not far from The Livery. During dinner he told me his amazing rags-to-riches story of how he became a successful publisher. After dinner, I paid the check and left the couple to finish their coffee and dessert as I rushed over to the Livery to meet and greet the attendees and make sure they put their name and contact information on our mailing list.

Melvin Powers, a charming and accomplished speaker, mesmerized the crowd. He had brought with him many copies of his books to give to those in attendance. After he spoke, his editor explained the importance of a well-edited book, whether a writer is looking for a publisher or plans to self-publish. She couldn't have chosen a better subject; it fit right into my plans. Surprisingly, nearly forty people attended the meeting and the donations came to more than enough to cover my expenses.

Later, SPAWN became a nonprofit 501(c)3 educational organization with monthly meetings in three different cities, Thousand Oaks, Ventura, and Santa Barbara, all run by volunteers. During the first few years we had interesting speakers at every meeting and drew a rather large attendance of from thirty to fifty people at each one. The suggested $5 donations we received helped pay our expenses to run the organization. I attended the meetings at each location every month, introducing the speaker and mentioning that I was a freelance editor. Some of the writers in the audience needed to find an editor and came up and spoke with me after the meeting. As a result of my involvement with SPAWN, I was launched as a freelance editor.

After a few years attendance fell off and we stopped having meetings. We went online with the organization and it is still serving a valuable service for writers with its website and online newsletter. Patricia Fry, who wrote about how she started as a freelance editor in Chapter 2 of this book, helped me with the organization from the beginning.

She became the Executive Director of SPAWN when I resigned and she still runs the organization.

In 2006 I produced a book festival which was held at my church. As there was no book festival in Ventura County I wanted to find out if there would be any interest. We had about 40 exhibitors and two or three hundred people attended. That went beyond my expectations. Some of the church members volunteered to help out; I could never have put it together by myself. As it was a church-sponsored event I didn't have to cover any of the expenses involved. They came out of the proceeds of over $3,000, all of which went to the church. Tom Berg, one of the leaders of the church, suggested that I form a nonprofit organization so that I could produce annual book festivals and get paid for my time. I said, "Good idea, and you can be cofounder." He agreed and the California Literary Arts Society (CLAS) was formed. To accommodate the large turnout, we moved the festival to a hotel right on the beach in Ventura and the Ventura Book Festival grew larger each year.

My involvement in these organizations has served to enhance my credentials as a writer, editor, and literary consultant. And the networking opportunities in producing a book festival are huge! I will be the first to admit that I have not done these things for purely altruistic reasons. However, writers and readers have also benefitted from the activities of both SPAWN and CLAS, so it has been a win-win situation.

Freelancing has provided me with a nice income all these years. I've been lucky. But it hasn't been luck alone. We freelancers need to make our presence known. Self-promotion through networking works wonders!

## BUILDING YOUR BUSINESS

Once you are ready for business you will want to be sure that anyone looking for an editor will be able to find you. One of the first things you should do is get a website that describes what you do, what your education and experience are, and some testimonials from satisfied clients. You may find it hard to ask the authors you have worked with to write something nice about you that you can put on your website and in brochures. At first I hesitated to do that but when I finally got up the courage to ask, I found that my clients were happy to write a short blurb expressing their appreciation for my expertise and my services. Many of them told me that without my help they would never have finished their book, much less get it published.

There are many reasons to stay on the good side of your clients. In addition to the obvious benefit of making your work more enjoyable both for you and the writer, it just makes good business sense. Happy clients will recommend you to others and will come back to you again with another project they are working on. Believe it or not, repeat business is not a rarity. Once someone gets the writing bug and produces a book they feel good about and that looks professional (with your help), they will want to write more "masterpieces."

## Brochures and business cards

If you are doing a lot of networking, you had better be ready to hand out business cards. There are several places on the Internet where you can choose one of their standard designs or design your own and then order professional-looking business cards. You can also have them done locally. Many printing companies will have someone on staff who will help you design your card. You can even design and print your cards yourself on your laser or inkjet printer. You can buy packages of card stock already scored so that they separate easily with smooth edges. There are some that can be printed on both sides. They usually come in packages that contain 200 to 250 cards, with ten cards to a sheet. Printing just a few cards at first might be a good idea until you have settled on just the right kind of card you should have, what you want to emphasize, and what information you want on it. Your card should clearly portray your services and provide contact information.

I usually print my own cards because some information might change before I use up the box of 100 to 500 cards I would get from a printing company. If you move, or change email addresses or Post Office box numbers—or even add valuable services that you want to promote, your business cards will be obsolete and you will have to order more. I use the type of cards that can be printed on both sides. One side of my cards contains information about my services. It has my company name, my name, telephone number, website, email address, and Post Office box number, and some brief information about what I do. On the other side of my cards I have the titles of some of the books I have written so that prospective clients will see not only what I do but will learn that I am also a published author and have written books about writing, editing, and publishing. This gives me additional credibility.

Some freelance editors have brochures that they can hand out at writing/publishing events or mail to those who inquire about their services. This is also a good promotional tool. If you know a good graphic designer and can afford her, you may want to get help with your brochure so that it has a professional look. If you don't want to spend the money for a designer and think you can do a good job of designing it yourself, there are packages of tri-fold brochure stock you can buy and you can design and print your own.

## Building and developing your own website

Having a website is also an excellent way to promote your services. It will help you as you promote your services on the Internet because you can create links to it for additional information.

You can hire a website designer or go to one of the free website design services on the Internet and do it yourself. Include a picture of yourself and detailed information about your services. If you have written books on writing or editing this is the place to list them. Be sure to include testimonials from happy clients. Of course, check with them first to see if they will agree to have their expressions of esteem and gratitude for your work posted for all to see.

As you build your business you can continue to develop your website, posting newsletters and articles you have written, and listing titles of books and other documents you have edited.

## Social Media

The social media can provide a boost to your business that traditional networking, promotion, and advertising strategies cannot match. The social network reaches millions of prospective clients. Two of the better-known online networking sites are Facebook (www.facebook. com) and Linkedin (www.linkedin.com). Both have the potential of promoting your services and boosting your client base. Better yet, you won't have to pay the high rates that you would if you were advertising in newspapers, magazines, and trade journals.

However, you should be cautious about becoming involved with social networks. According to a Consumer Reports (CR) survey, "More than five million U.S. households experienced some type of abuse on Facebook in the past year [2010], including virus infections and identity theft." They report that the online threats are at high levels, with a third of consumers experiencing malicious software infection causing them to replace 1.3 million PCs in 2010. You can guard against some of the threats, however, by using security software. There is free anti-malware available which should provide protection for many people. The top two recommendations by CR are Avira, AntiVir Personal (free-av.com) and AVG Anti-Virus Free Edition 2011, (free.avg.com). Also, Facebook has privacy controls, and even though they might not prevent every breach, they definitely help.

### Facebook

Facebook is the largest online social network—as of this writing. However, things change so fast with some companies and organizations going out of business and other, larger ones taking their place that you will need to do the research yourself when you are ready to take part in them. On Facebook you can set up an Official Page for any type of business, organization, or service to reach your target market, let them know what services you provide, and get feedback. And setting up your Facebook page is free. For a small fee you can set up an ad that targets users based on profile data so that you can reach those who may be most interested in your message.

Their business accounts are designed for those who only want to use the site to administer Pages and their ad campaigns. They do not have the same functionality as personal accounts. According to the Facebook website, an individual with a business account can view all the Pages and Social Ads that they have created but they won't be able to view the profiles of users on the site or other content on the site that does not live on the Pages they administer. Business accounts cannot be found in search and cannot send or receive friend requests. For more information go to their website, www.facebook.com.

*LinkedIn*

LinkedIn is about B2B (business-to-business) so some consider it the better choice for interacting with suppliers and partners and improving business communications and sales. When you become a member, your company profile contains information about the industry you serve, key demographics, and tells prospects what benefits they will receive if they choose your services. Through LinkedIn you can join groups or associations that can offer valuable network connections.

Information on their website states that roughly one million new members join LinkedIn every week, at a rate equivalent to a professional joining the site faster than one member per second. LinkedIn claims to be the world's largest professional network on the Internet with more than 100 million members in over 200 countries and territories. They state that there were nearly two billion people searches on LinkedIn in 2010.

*Twitter*

Then there is Twitter (www.twitter.com), which is a real-time information network that connects you to information that you find interesting. As their website explains it, Twitter contains small bursts of information called Tweets. Each Tweet is 140 characters in length, and connected to each Tweet is a details pane that provides additional information. You can tell your story within your Tweet, or you can think of a Tweet as the headline, and use the details pane to tell the rest with photos, videos, and other media content.

Whether or not you Tweet, you still have access to the voices and information surrounding what interests you. You can contribute, or just listen in.

Twitter connects businesses to customers in real-time. Businesses use it to quickly share information with people interested in their products and services, gather real-time market intelligence and feed-back, and build relationships with customers, partners, and influential people.

There are many other social networking sites that can help your busi-ness. One of them is Yelp (www.yelp.com). It is also a mobile app with networks in all fifty states and eight countries. As it is specifically focused on local businesses, members can share their opinions on the places they go to or services they receive personally.

Another site is Biznik (www.biznik.com), which is aimed at small business owners, entrepreneurs, and single-owner companies, helping them to make and maintain connections with each other.

*Blogging*

This is another way to get the word out about your services. Be clear about who you are and what services you provide. An informational blog can help you establish your credibility and build a relationship of trust with potential clients. A business blog should have a specific func-tion. Every blog you write should be relevant and interesting to your target audience. You will also have to keep updating your blog to keep it fresh and current. Take a look at other business blogs to see how they have been written. That will give you some ideas about how to write yours.

As technology changes rapidly and new sites are popping up all the time, you will need to keep yourself informed to find out which of them will work best for you and provide the maximum potential of reaching writers who will be interested in your services.

# ☙5☙

## *Working with an Author*

Much of what follows refers to a book manuscript that you receive directly from an author, not a publisher, although the basic principles are the same no matter what is being edited or who hired you to do it.

### AT THE BEGINNING

When you get the manuscript, tell the author that you want to look it over before you begin so that you can be sure that it is ready to be edited. This will allow you to get an idea of the subject matter and how it is presented. You can also determine the kind of editing that needs to be done. A quick read-through will reveal the nature of the material and the potential audience for it.

Once you accept the job, ask the author to register his copyright before you start work on his manuscript. That will protect the author if any of the information falls into the wrong hands and someone else tries to claim ownership of it. Some authors may ask you to sign a non-disclosure agreement. Even though it has always been my policy not to discuss a client's manuscript or her ideas anyway, I want to put the author at ease so I am happy to sign such an agreement.

Ideas are not protected by copyright, which only protects the concrete expression of an idea. And sometimes an idea has great commercial value and needs to be kept confidential so that someone else cannot use it and reap the benefits. Often the author will have her attorney draw up the agreement and it is important for you to read it carefully to be sure that you agree to it. I have not received one nondisclosure agreement that I would not agree to sign. Most of them state simply that I will keep the information confidential, which I do as a matter of course.

Here is a sample nondisclosure agreement.

## Nondisclosure Agreement for Submitting Ideas

**W**hat can be more frustrating than having a great idea and not being able to share it with anyone? If the idea has commercial value, sharing it is often the first step on the way to realizing the remunerative potential of the concept. The author wants to show the idea to a publisher, manufacturer, or producer. But how can the idea be protected?

Ideas are not protected by copyright, because copyright only protects the concrete expression of an idea. The idea to write a guide to the White House is not copyrightable, but the written guide certainly is protected by copyright. The idea to have a television series in which each program would have a narrator teach local history at a well-known landmark in his or her locale is not copyrightable, but each program would be protected by copyright. Of course, copyright is not the only form of legal protection. An idea might be patentable or lead to the creation of a trademark, but such cases are less likely and certainly require expert legal assistance. How does an author disclose an idea for an image, a format, a product, or other creations without risking that the listener, or potential business associate, will simply steal the idea?

This can be done by the creation of an express contract, an implied contract (revealed by the course of dealing between the parties), or a fiduciary relationship (in which one party owes a duty of trust to the other party). Form 11, the Nondisclosure Agreement, creates an express contract between the party disclosing the idea and the party receiving it. Form 11 is adapted from a letter agreement in *Licensing Art & Design* by Caryn Leland (Allworth Press).

What should be done if a company refuses to sign a nondisclosure agreement or, even worse, has its own agreement for the author to sign? Such an agreement might say that the company will not be liable for using a similar idea and will probably place a maximum value on the idea (such as a few hundred dollars). At this point, the author has to evaluate the risk. Does the company have a good reputation or is it notorious for appropriating ideas? Are there other companies that could be approached with the idea, ones that would be willing to sign a nondisclosure agreement? If not, taking the risk may make more sense than never exploiting the idea at all. A number of steps, set out in the negotiation checklist, should then be taken to try and gain some protection. The author will have to make these evaluations on a case-by-case basis.

### Filling in the Form

In the Preamble fill in the date and the names and addresses of the parties. In Paragraph 1 describe the information to be disclosed without giving away what it is. Have both parties sign the agreement.

### Negotiation Checklist

❑ Disclose what the information concerns without giving away what is new or innovative. For example, "an idea for a new format for a series to teach history" might interest a producer but would not give away the particulars of the idea (i.e., using different narrators teaching at landmarks in different locales). (Paragraph 1)

❑ State that the recipient is reviewing the information to decide whether to embark on commercial exploitation. (Paragraph 2)

❑ Require the recipient to agree not to use or transfer the information. (Paragraph 3)

❏ State that the recipient receives no rights in the information. (Paragraph 3)

❏ Require the recipient to keep the information confidential. (Paragraph 4)

❏ State that the recipient acknowledges that disclosure of the information would cause irreparable harm to the author. (Paragraph 4)

❏ Require good faith negotiations if the recipient wishes to use the information after disclosure. (Paragraph 5)

❏ Allow no use of the information unless agreement is reached after such good faith negotiations. (Paragraph 5)

If the author wishes to disclose the information despite the other party's refusal to sign the author's nondisclosure form, the author should take a number of steps:

❏ First, before submission, the idea should be sent to a neutral third party (such as a notary public or professional authors' society) to be held in confidence.

❏ Anything submitted should be marked with copyright and trademark notices, when appropriate. For example, the idea may not be copyrightable, but the written explanation of the idea certainly is. The copyright notice could be for that explanation, but might make the recipient more hesitant to steal the idea.

❏ If an appointment is made, confirm it by letter in advance and sign any log for visitors.

❏ After any meeting, send a letter that covers what happened at the meeting (including any disclosure of confidential information and any assurances that information will be kept confidential) and, if at all possible, have any proposal or followup from the recipient be in writing.

Then factor in the time required to examine the manuscript and tell the author that you will be including that charge in your invoice. It shouldn't take very long to briefly scan the document and determine if you have enough to go forward. Don't assume that the author knows how you work. By explaining everything you will be doing in as much detail as you can from the very beginning, you will avoid some misunderstandings down the road.

If your career goes the way mine has, you will be receiving manuscripts from your clients by mail, by attachments to an email, or through your clients delivering them to you in person. I like the in-person delivery because I get to meet the writer personally and that helps establish a friendly working relationship with her or him. However, I have had many clients who I have never met, as they lived far away.

Sometimes after only a quick look at the manuscript you may be able to point out some problems or things you will want to have the writer change before you start editing. You may find that the manuscript isn't even close to being ready for editing. In that case, it's best to explain what more the author has to do, being as specific as possible, and then hand the manuscript back. If you try to edit a manuscript that isn't ready, and many clients will want you to, it will take a much longer time to do it. And the manuscript might have to be re-edited after the author has reworked it. It's best that he fix the problems before you begin. Both for you and for the client. It will save him money, and will save you some anguish. Believe me, in the long run your client will be grateful and your relationship won't become strained.

## MANUSCRIPT PREPARATION

The author has the responsibility of getting the manuscript to you in good shape and as complete as possible, to that point. It should include all of the parts of the book or a list of the parts that are missing. What is essential for you to have from the beginning are the title page, a preface or introduction (if there will be any), and any important back matter such as a glossary or appendixes.

If the edited manuscript is to be presented to a publisher or literary agent or will be sent to a book designer it should be formatted according to the publisher's manuscript-preparation guidelines. The following guidelines will explain how to do that. This, I believe, is one of the editor's responsibilities to the author.

---

## GUIDELINES FOR AUTHORS

### The Manuscript

Please provide a file and a hard copy of the manuscript. The file must be saved in a standard format (recent versions of Microsoft Word or as a rich text format [.rtf] file). If this is a difficulty, *please call to ensure that we will be able to read the files.*

The manuscript should be complete. Information, including bibliographic information and appendixes, should not be left incomplete, unless clearly marked

---

on the pages. With regard to the formatting of the manuscript files, please note the following:

- If you are new to computers, please ask someone to show you how simple it is to use word wrap—that is, allowing the word processing program to wrap your words through to the next line without interruption. Do not use the computer as a typewriter and put carriage returns after each line.
- Manuscripts should be double-spaced with one-inch margins. Do not use condensed type or any special typefaces. ALWAYS use Times New Roman (or Times or Times Roman), because these fonts seem to translate cross platform fluidly (i.e., from your Mac to our PC; from our PC to the designer's page layout software). Other fonts often cause proofreading nightmares due to translation problems (hyphens become = signs, quotes become capital A's and @ marks, and so on).
- Do not create complex style sheets in Word—in fact, we much prefer it if you do not work with style sheets at all. Use one style—12 point times new roman type, double spaced, justified left, rag right—throughout. If you need to style your heads bold, or you want to add italic for emphasis, or you need to put text in a block, etc.,—please do these things *manually*, not through style sheets.
- Justify text to the left margin only.
- The fewer commands in the file, the better. In the running text, do not underline for emphasis; do not bold (except for heads and subheads); do not capitalize entire words. You can use italic.
- Do not put more than one space between sentences.
- Do not skip an extra line space between paragraphs. Indent paragraphs instead, except as described in bullet point below.
- Do not indent the first paragraph of a chapter, or the first paragraph below a subhead; these should all be flush left.
- The title of the chapter should be flush left, in bold and include the number of the chapter. A chapter title looks like this:

**Chapter 6: Principles of Business Automation**

- Subheads are the titles that divide a chapter into parts. They are hierarchical. So for example, if the chapter title is "Chapter 6: Principles of Business Automation," the first subhead is "Coping with the Photographers Lifestyle." We call that an A head, because it is the first (hierarchical) level of heads below the chapter title. But underneath that there are a number of B heads. They are "Hiring Help Won't Always Do" and "A New Way to Think about Using Computers" and "A Business Automation Solution." All of these topics fall within the subject area described by the A head, so they are subsidiary to it, and all are B heads. Almost all nonfiction books have some division of material within chapters, so most of them will have A heads. Not all books will need further levels of heads—it is up to you to make that decision.

- Here is how you should designate heads. To indicate which is which, heads need to be labeled and lightly styled, as follows. A-heads should be consistently bold flush left, and B-heads should be consistently bold indented. If you have C subsubsubheads, they should be indented and styled as bold italic: Labeling the level of the head is more important than styling it.

## The Main Chapter Title

Use a subhead for each new subject. In addition each subhead should be indicated like this:

### A Lovely A Subhead

Then you should have running text below the A head, before you have a B head, because we don't like to have heads directly below heads.

#### *Or If You Need a B Subsubhead*

Blah, blah, blah, more running text. . . until perhaps you find you need another level of heads in which case you would have to resort to using a C subsubsubhead, which looks like this.

##### THIS WOULD BE THE C HEAD

Continue with the running text.

Please remember *IT IS NOT YOUR JOB TO DESIGN THE MANUSCRIPT ON YOUR COMPUTER*, but it is your job to set up the structure of the manuscript clearly so that others can create a design. If you have any question about what subheads are and how to use the subheads, please call and speak to us.

A subhead should occur about every two hundred words (roughly once per double-spaced page).

- Skip a space before subheads.
- As regards sidebars (more about this below), bulleted and numbered lists,

forms inserted into the text, in short anything that interrupts the regular running text, make sure that you mark it clearly again using the **[square brackets]** method denoted above in the section on subheads. So for example, at the beginning of a special form inserted into the running text, you would type **[begin form]** and at the end you would type **[end form]**. Or if, for example, you have boxed text, you can mark it **[begin boxed text]** before and **[end boxed text]** at the end.

• Use the spellcheck on all text.

## Use of Images

If your book is going to contain illustrated materials (i.e. photographs, charts, graphs, and so on), you should let us know how many there are and where these items will need to be placed. We will accept images in multiple formats (digital, black and white prints, transparencies, etc.), but please let us know in advance what formats you plan to use. If you are using digital images our printer has specifications as to file size, resolution, and type of file. We can work with jpegs, Tiffs, eps files, PDFs, but it's important that the image have enough resolution for print. This generally means that the image has to be 300 dpi, at printed size. If you are using digital images, *NOTE THAT THE IMAGE FILES SHOULD NOT BE EMBEDDED IN THE TEXT.* Digital images need to be sent to us on a separate disk. Make sure that you number all images and that the number corresponds to: (1) a numbered caption, if one is necessary, and (2) a place marker in the text.

For example, if you are using slides in your book, you should number the slides 1, 2, 3, 4, etc. Then, in the text at the appropriate place you should insert the marker **[insert slide 1 here]** When the typesetter goes through the file, he will be able to substitute the correct image for the correct place marker.

If you are using digital files, please make sure that the file name corresponds to the place marker in the text. If your file is called girl2.tif, make sure that the place marker in the file says **[insert girl2.tif].**

It is extremely important that pictures are named or numbered and that the system of naming or numbering is *exactly* the same on the picture or file *and* in the text. Remember, the typesetter is not familiar with your book, and he is not going to be able to figure out which images go where without very specific guidance from you.

One other issue regarding pictures, which doesn't really belong here, because it's not about style, but it is very important. If you are using images, make sure that you have the *right* to use those images. For example, if you resolve to use a full page illustration by a prominent living artist without getting his permission, you are making a very bad decision. If you want to use a photograph you took of a model, and she never signed a release, better contact her now, and get her to sign that release. This stuff can be sticky; call if you have questions and we will offer guidance.

## Style

Matters of style should, for the most part, follow *The Chicago Manual of Style,* sixteenth edition, and *Webster's Collegiate Dictionary,* eleventh edition. Be consistent in all matters of style and spelling. Make a style sheet in which you resolve all questions of style and spelling, such as names (which should be fact-checked) or words that are not in the dictionary (e.g., technical terms or terminology particular to your subject). Turn in this style sheet with the manuscript so we can benefit from it.

Keep to the agreed-upon page count for the book. Please ask any questions you may have, since the ultimate production of the book will be greatly aided by following these guidelines.

## Some General Matters of Style

- Paragraphs should rarely run longer than half a page.
- Make sure that the table of contents matches the text. Often the chapter titles appear one way in the contents and another in the chapter itself (the same goes for subheads).
- Always use the serial comma—that is, for items in a series, always put a comma after the last item before "and" or "or" (e.g., A, B, and C).
- Em dashes should have no spaces on either side (e.g., fish—small, medium, and large). If you have not created a shortcut key in order to insert em dashes, please use a double dash—which will convert easily to a proper em dash.
- There is no space before or after a forward slash.
- Watch for which/that confusion.
- Watch for noun/pronoun agreement (e.g., do not refer to a company as "them" or use "they" when referring to one person). In cases of political-correctness with regard to gender, try to alternate examples from paragraph to paragraph or from case to case (it is often a good idea to assign genders to particular hypothetical examples and use them consistently throughout the manuscript—"the musician" is consistently referred to as "he," "the lawyer" is consistently referred to as "she," and so on).

- Always spell out the word "and" in running text (and even in bulleted lists), unless it is the case that an ampersand appears as a part of a company's legitimate name.
- Spell out the word "versus" unless citing a legal case.
- The words "street," "avenue," "boulevard," or "suite" should be spelled out in addresses.

## Chapters and Subheads

- Chapter titles and all levels of subheads should be in title case (i.e., have initial letters of each word capitalized, except for articles, prepositions, and connectives). The first letter of the first and last word should always be capitalized.
- Don't start chapters with subheads. The first subhead should always follow a block of text introducing the chapter.
- When referring to another chapter in the book, use numerals for the chapter numbers and do not capitalize the word "chapter" (e.g., see chapter 14). The same goes for appendixes (e.g., appendix B). Cross-references between chapters should be filled in when the manuscript is handed in.

## Lists and Text Boxes

- Use text boxes sparingly, if necessary. Usually, material can be organized by separating it into paragraphs dividing it with A- or B-heads. Stories, examples, checklists, and forms lend themselves to boxes and "sidebars." These should not be less than seventy-five words or more than a book page and never more than a two-page spread.
- If you wish to box certain text, indicate this in the manuscript by typing **[begin box]** at the start of the box, and **[end box]** where it concludes. Text in a box should be able to stand by itself and should not be fixed as to where it falls in the chapter.
- Avoid long lists.
- For short lists, use bullets—but try not to do so often. A short bulleted list is often better run together as a paragraph.
- Only number lists if the numbering makes the list easier to understand (such as with a series of steps to be taken). If you are numbering, do not then use lettering for a later list.
- The first letter of a list item is always capitalized, even if the list is a grammatical continuation of the introductory sentence.

- If the reader might want to check off items, it is possible to make checklists by using boxes that can be checked rather than bullets.

## Italics versus Quotation Marks
- In addition to specific matters of emphasis, italics are used for: titles of books, periodicals, works of art, long poems and musical compositions, titles of exhibitions, and foreign words or phrases not in the dictionary.
- "Words as words" (e.g., definitions) are set in quotation marks.
- "Letters as letters" are set in italics (e.g., the letter r).
- If a periodical or newspaper title begins with the word "the," it should not be capitalized or set in italics (e.g., the *New York Times,* the *New Yorker).*
- Books, films, and works of art with titles beginning with the word "the" should be set in all italics and title case (e.g., *The Artist's Guide to New Markets*).
- Articles published in periodicals are set in quotation marks.
- Do not use the words "so-called" before words in quotation marks.

## Numbers
- Numbers one to one hundred should be spelled out.
- Ages are spelled out (sixty-five years old).
- Use numerals for percentages in running text, with the word "percent" spelled out (75 percent)
- Amounts in dollars should be left in numerals with the dollar sign in front ($25.00, or simply $25). This applies to other currency as well (£50, or ¥1,000).
- Always use a comma with numerals unless otherwise instructed (e.g., shutter speeds of camera equipment are typically left without commas).

## Dialogue
- Interior, unspoken, or imagined dialogue are not set in quotation marks, unless to avoid confusion. This is also the case for maxims, proverbs, and familiar expressions.
- When a quotation runs over the course of more than one paragraph and the speaker remains the same, quotation marks are placed at the beginning, but not at the end, of each paragraph, and then at the end of the quote.
- When there is a quotation within a quotation, use single quotes.

### Spelling

The following words are not in the dictionary and are spelled as follows:

- Internet (also: the Net)
- website (also: the Web)
- email
- zine
- online/offline

### The Index

By contract, you are required to provide us with an index for your book. Although many word processing programs have an indexing option, unfortunately, you will not be able to use this to create your index. Rather, you will have to wait until the book is designed and in galley pages, and then provide a separate, alphabetized file, containing the indexed topics, and the page numbers as listed in the galleys. If you are new to indexing, *The Chicago Manual of Style* provides detailed instructions as to how to index in Chapter 17. If you choose not to provide an index (many authors do not), we will outsource the galleys to a professional indexer, and that charge will be held against your royalties.

### Fact Checking

We do not have a fact-checking department. Although our copyeditors and proofreaders do a valiant job of double-checking, you are ultimately responsible for making sure that dates are correct, names and foreign words are spelled correctly, images are properly captioned, credited, cropped, and aligned, and so on.

Some of your clients will be self-publishing and some will be looking for a publisher—or a literary agent—and authors need to present a polished manuscript so that they can have the best possible chance of getting published. In the present economic climate where profits have been declining dramatically, publishers don't wish to spend a lot of time and money on extensive editing of a manuscript even when they like the subject matter. When they see a well organized, articulate manuscript that fits their catalog they are bound to sit up and take notice. If it has also been professionally edited according to book publishing standards they are more likely to take it on than they would another equally impressive one that needs a lot of work. And it isn't just because they know it will cost less to whip it into shape for publishing, a well edited book is easier to read and comprehend, which makes it more appealing to readers. This kind of book will likely sell enough copies to make the publisher a profit. And making a profit is the number one reason they are in business.

## DETERMINING WHICH CLIENTS TO TAKE

Your time is valuable and not all potential clients understand that. I have learned not to take on a client who says, "You won't have to do much editing. I have already edited the book." Few writers can edit their own work. In Susan Page's book, *The Shortest Distance Between You and a Published Book,* she states, "Writing is a two-person job. Even if you are a skilled editor of your own work, a second skilled editor will make suggestions you will inevitably miss, simply because, as the author, you lose a certain amount of objectivity."

Sometimes the author has had her book edited by a friend who is a teacher or writer or someone who might be knowledgeable about English usage, grammar, and so forth but has not had any training in editing a book. This potential client may not be prepared to pay for the time it will take to bring her manuscript up to professional book publishing standards. Often the author thinks it looks fine and doesn't want to believe she wasted her money. In my evaluation and critique I point out the errors and tell her it must be edited by someone who understands all of the principles of editing books before it is ready to submit to a publisher or literary agent—or even to self-publish.

It is a difficult situation when the author has brought it to me for my professional opinion and for help in doing a final polish. When I explain that it could take many hours to edit her book properly, she is crestfallen. Unless she can see for herself that the manuscript needs a lot of work, I am reluctant to take it on. A job like that is fraught with pitfalls.

How do you determine whether you should work with a particular client? During the first few years of working as a freelance editor, I would sometimes accept a job that I had serious reservations about. As I don't advertise or do much promoting of my services, there have been times when work was slow and, frankly, I needed the income. I learned, however, that if I took work that wasn't ready to be edited, I would later regret it. This happened to me only twice in my career. In both cases I realized the work needed a complete rewrite. It wasn't focused; it wasn't complete with a beginning, middle, and end; the subject matter was unclear; or the writing was so muddy that I couldn't understand what the author was trying to say. In each case I made suggestions to the author as to how to better organize the material. They asked me to work on it as it was and, going against my intuition or common sense, I did.

I asked for an advance before I started and I deposited their check before I completed the first phase of the process, which was to edit the first few pages so that they could see if what I was doing met with their approval. When I returned the edited pages, I asked them to make some specific changes before I continued. They begged me to continue anyway and I did, but without payment in advance for the next phase. However, I told them that I would want to be paid upon presentation of the next phase of the edited manuscript. I continued because they had said that they liked what I had done, and I knew I could make their writing better than it was when I got it. Besides, their first check had cleared so the next one should, too, shouldn't it?

At this point I have to say that it wasn't just their poor writing that made me wary of taking the job. It was something about the client that I didn't trust but I couldn't put my finger on it so I thought it was just my imagination.

In the first case, when I gave the client the next phase of the work I had completed and submitted an invoice, she said she would send me the check later. She had forgotten her checkbook. After a couple of weeks, I called her and she said the check was in the mail. I'd heard that one before. Well, the short version of this story is that she never paid me. I suppose I could have hounded her for payment but I didn't bother. At that point I never wanted to talk to her again. But I made a mental note to listen to my inner voice which had kept saying *don't take this job!*

I don't always follow my own good advice, and it was a few years later when another job ended in a similar way. I called the client asking for payment and he said that he had shown my edits to a friend of his and his friend said that I'd made a lot of mistakes in the editing. He cited a few examples and in every case, his friend was wrong. My changes were accurate; his friend was full of, well, you know. Or maybe there was no "friend" and my client just didn't want to pay me and made the story up. At any event, he never paid me.

I trusted these clients when I had a feeling that I shouldn't. I haven't made those mistakes again. I listen to my inner voice now. I refuse all work that needs an extensive rewrite and I turn away all clients I just don't want to work with—for any reason. That's the beauty of being freelance. I can do that. You might ask why I didn't take these deadbeat clients to small claims court but I decided I didn't want to spend the time it would take and I just wanted to forget about it and move on. Fortunately, it wasn't a lot of money because I had had enough sense not to put much time into the second phase of their work before I sent them an invoice.

## ESTIMATING TIME

When the author brings his manuscript to me, he will usually want to know how much time it will take and what the charges might be. However, this information is impossible to estimate until I have had a chance to work for a while on the manuscript. I would discourage an editor from editing a few pages of a book manuscript free of charge in order to give the author an idea of how she edits and how long it might take for the entire project. You would have to edit at least 10 percent of the manuscript to determine with some accuracy the time involved.

If there were a lot of additional materials such as an index, glossary of terms, endnotes, and a bibliography, they would take additional time. It would be impossible to estimate how much time those pages would take to edit, as there are certain styles and procedures that must be followed, and each item would have to be checked for accuracy. They usually take longer to edit, per page, than the main text.

Some editors will offer to edit a few pages for a mutually agreed number of hours which the author will pay for in advance, to see how many pages she was able to edit during that time period. I always offer that procedure to my potential clients as the only way to be able to make an educated guess at what the total costs might be. As I always charge by the hour for editing, I usually ask for an advance to cover, say, four hours of my time. When I return the edited material to the author, he can see, based on the number of pages I edited in that amount of time, how long the rest of the text might take to edit. He can also see if he likes what I did up to that point and determine whether he wants to go forward.

For example, if one edited for four hours at the rate of five pages an hour and the manuscript was 200 double-spaced pages, it would take about forty hours to edit the main text. If the editor charged $50 per hour, the total charges could be estimated as around $2,000. These charges would not include the front matter or back matter of the book, only the text. This should be stated at the beginning. If you have done a lot of editing of bibliographies, glossaries, and other such matter you may be able to make an estimate of how long they will take to edit. But the likelihood is that bibliographies will take longer than straight text and glossaries will take less time. You will have to consider the number of entries on each page and whether you will have to change the formatting or styles.

I have had several 500-plus page books to edit and since they take several months to do, I invoice monthly for work I have done to that point. This works well for most writers because they can spread out their payments over time. Also, because I often work for two or more clients at a time, I can make progress on each of their books rather than have a client wait several months to get started. It works for me, too, because I can accommodate both clients that way. And being paid monthly gives me a fairly steady income for the duration of the jobs.

## THE STRUCTURE OF A BOOK

To work effectively with authors of book manuscripts, the editor must be able to help him with the format, layout, and organization of his work. We have to know how to arrange a book, which includes the beginning, middle, and end as well as the order in which the parts of the book should be presented. Most of the authors I work with do not know the divisions of a book and what comes first. Editors who can edit other types of writing very well but rarely work with book authors are not likely to know that either. This is another area where the *Chicago Manual of Style* comes in handy.

Often neither the writer nor editor even think of the front or back parts of the book until the text is finished. And that's because it might not be clear what those parts should entail until then. The need for some parts, like an index or glossary, might not be determined until the entire text has been written and edited. The editor, however, should have them in mind as she is editing because the front and back matter can take a great deal of time to do, especially if the author doesn't know how to write and/or compile them and asks the editor to take on that chore. If the editor needs to explain the structure of a book and guide the author through the process of preparing it, the additional charges for time might be considerably more than the editor originally estimated. The author should be apprised of this as soon as it becomes apparent.

I believe it's best to overestimate the charges at the beginning just in case something like this happens during the course of editing. Otherwise it can cause hard feelings between the author and editor. It can even cause the author to mistrust the editor, and this is a relationship where trust is paramount. The author who "gave birth" to the book puts the welfare of her "baby" into the hands of the editor to nurture it and prepare it to meet the world. The book's author needs to be comfortable with what the editor is doing with her creation as well as what it is going to cost. She should never feel that she is being overcharged. Everything about the process should be revealed to the author as soon as possible. There should never be any surprises.

All books have what is called "front matter," which usually consists of a title page, a copyright page, table of contents, and acknowledgments. A novel may not have what is called "back matter" except for perhaps a bio of the author. But a nonfiction book could have several sections of back matter. What follows is an explanation of the organization of a book.

## THE DIVISIONS OF A BOOK

The trimmed sheets of paper in a book are called leaves and a page is one side of a leaf. The front of the leaf, which lies to the right of an open book, is called the recto. The back of the leaf, which lies on the left side of an open book after a page is turned, is called the verso. Rectos are always odd-numbered pages and versos are even-numbered pages.

There are three major divisions to the interior of a book: the front matter, or preliminaries; the text; and the back matter, also called end matter or reference matter. The three main divisions are comprised of several parts. Not all books contain all three divisions or parts.

## FRONT MATTER

The front matter of a book can consist of a combination of any of the following. I have not described all of them, only the ones that are generally used. Many books do not contain a half-title page or many of the other parts listed below. The list is in order of appearance in the book. Although they can be arranged differently, this will provide a guide as to where they would ordinarily go.

Book half-title
Series title, frontispiece, or blank

Title page
Copyright page
Dedication
Epigraph
Table of Contents
List of Illustrations
List of Tables
Foreword
Preface
Acknowledgments
Introduction (if not part of text)
Abbreviations (if not in back matter)
Chronology (if not in back matter)

## Title Page

Front matter for books can include a half-title page on the first recto (right-hand page) which consists only of the main title. The verso (the other side or left-hand page) of the half-title page could be blank or carry an illustration (called a *frontispiece*) or something else.

Next comes the title page which shows the full title of the book; the subtitle, if any; the name of the author, editor, or translator; and the name and location of the publisher.

## Copyright Page

The verso of the title page is called the copyright page which carries information on the book, such as the following (but not necessarily in this order):

- A copyright notice that shows the year copyrighted and the owner of the copyright—usually the author. Example: © 2011 by Mary Embree. Some contain the name of the organization that published the book: © 2010 by the University of Chicago. This may be followed by the statement, "All rights reserved.

No part of this book may be reproduced, stored in a retrieval system, or transmitted in any form, or by any means, electronic, mechanical, photocopying, recording or otherwise, without prior permission of the publisher."

- The publisher's name and address
- Publishing history, such as the edition number:

First edition published in 1906. Sixteenth edition published in 2010

- Library of Congress Catalog Number (LCCN) or Library of Congress Cataloging-in-Publication (CIP) data. The LCCN is used mostly by small publishers and self-publishers while the CIP is used by publishers of multiple books.
- The International Standard Book Number (ISBN). This uniquely identifies the book, provides ordering information, and assists in inventory tracking. This number should also be printed on the book cover or jacket. Each format or binding (hardcover, paperback, CD-ROM, e-book, etc.) must have a separate ISBN.
- The country of printing

Some copyright pages also contain a mention of the cover designer or book designer. Front matter also might include acknowledgments, the dedication, table of contents, a foreword, and a preface. Unless an editor is working directly with an established book publisher or very knowledgeable author, the above information is important for her to know, as she may be guiding the author in the total production of his book.

The following parts of a book might not be in every book but they are important to know so that you, the editor, can inform the author of them.

## Dedication

If there is a dedication, it appears on a page by itself directly after the copyright page, usually on the recto (right-hand page.) The word "dedicated" is not necessary. This example is from *The Color of Water* by James McBride:

> I wrote this book for my mother,
> and her mother,
> and mothers everywhere.

## Epigraph

An epigraph is a quotation that is relevant to the text. It is usually placed on the verso, opposite the table of contents. Epigraphs are sometimes used as chapter openings as well. The source of the quotation is given on a line following it, sometimes preceded by an em dash. Here is an example:

> The difference between the right word and the almost right word . . . is the difference between the lightning and the lightning bug.
>
> —Mark Twain

## Table of Contents

The table of contents begins on a right-hand page. It should include all of the preliminary material that follows it. It lists the title and beginning page number of each section of the book and the back matter, such as the index and illustrations.

## Foreword

This is written by someone other than the author. The name of the foreword's author may appear at the end, often flush right, and the title or affiliation of the author may appear under the name.

## Preface

This is the author's own statement about the book. It includes reasons for writing the book, method of research, and sometimes permissions granted for the use of previously published material. The author might sign it with just his initials, as it is understood that it was written by the author.

## Acknowledgments

This may be a separate section following the preface. Often, this is where the author thanks the people who have helped him or made some contribution to the information in the book.

## Introduction

This may or may not be included in front matter. It is more common now to make this as part of the text, with pagination in Arabic numerals like the rest of the text. If the introduction is by someone other than the author, it is included in the front matter.

## BACK MATTER

Back matter can consist of any of the following. I have described in detail only the ones most often used.

Acknowledgments (if not in front matter)
Appendix or appendixes
Chronology (if not in front matter)
Abbreviations (if not in front matter)
Notes
Glossary
Bibliography or References
List of Contributors

Illustration Credits (if not in captions or elsewhere)

Index or indexes

## Appendixes

Please note that this is spelled *appendixes*, not *appendices* in *The Chicago Manual of Style*. And if the *Manual* says it is correct, then who are we to question it? Use the old spelling only if you wish to appear dated. It's important to update your terminology.

An appendix may include explanations that are not necessary to the text but contain clarifications, texts of documents, long lists, or charts and tables. Appendixes usually follow the last chapter of the book. When there are two or more appendixes, they should be given a title and designated by numbers (Appendix 1, Appendix 2, etc.) or letters (Appendix A, Appendix B, etc.).

## Chronology

This can be placed in either the front matter or back matter. But if this information is particularly helpful to the reader in following the story from the beginning, it is best placed in the front matter. In biographies, memoirs, historical fiction, and other types of books where it is easy to get confused about what happened, when it happened, and to whom it happened, a chronology can help straighten all that out.

## Notes; Endnotes

These follow the appendix and precede the bibliography or reference list. Endnotes are sometimes placed at the end of the chapters to which they refer.

## Glossary

I really like glossaries, especially if there are unfamiliar words and terms in a book. It is also a useful tool when a book contains a lot technological, scientific, or foreign words. The words should be in alphabetical order, each on a separate line, and followed by its definition. A glossary usually precedes a bibliography or reference list.

## Bibliography or References

These are usually set in smaller type than the text. The editor should know the style used for bibliographies, as styles used in books are different from styles used in other kinds of writing, such as dissertations. Style books for the field in which they are working are absolutely essential for freelance editors. For help with bibliographies, check the *Chicago Manual* for examples of them.

## Index

*The Chicago Manual* states, "In a book with both name and subject indexes, the name index should precede the subject index." Thus, there could be two or more indexes in a book. However, in most of the books I have seen, including the ones I have written, both names and subjects are in a single index.

Not many authors know how to prepare an index or have the time to do it. In fact, not many editors have the technical skills to prepare a good index. Indexing is a specialty and it should be done by a person who is widely read, detail oriented, analytical, knowledgeable about publishing practices, and able to handle tight deadlines. The indexer, of course, should be very familiar with the subject matter and do the indexing with the potential reader in mind.

Indexing is a skill that you, as an editor, could learn to do and it would greatly enhance your value to an author and/or publisher. *The Chicago Manual* has a comprehensive chapter on indexes in the latest (16th) edition. It covers the following:

- Components of an Index
- General Principles of Indexing

- Indexing Proper Name and Variants
- Indexing Titles of Publications and Other Works
- Alphabetizing
- Punctuation Indexes
- The Mechanics of Indexing
- Editing an Index Compiled by Someone Else
- Typographical Considerations for Indexes
- Examples of Indexes

There are computer programs that can help you enormously in preparing an index. In Microsoft Word, it explains how to mark and customize each entry. Since each new edition of Word is slightly different (and sometimes a lot different) I won't go into the procedure here. But it is explained in their Help and How-to section on creating an index. After you have marked each entry, you will go to the end of the document and click on where you want to insert the finished index. The entire list appears in two columns with page numbers indicating where each entry is found. When you figure it all out, it is like magic and it saves you a lot of time.

If you are preparing an index for a book publisher, they will not want you to put the page numbers in the index. In fact, you probably won't even be able to use the indexing program built into your word-processing system. It still can help though because it will serve as a guide when you retype the index and add the appropriate page numbers.

The publisher will be designing the pages for a book of a certain size, such as five-and-a-half by eight-and-a-half inches, six by nine inches or some other size. They will have to reformat the manuscript, changing the font style and size, adding titles and page numbers to the top and/or bottom of the pages, and other features found in printed books. Thus, the page numbers will change and that means the index will have the wrong page numbers listed. If you are the indexer, they will send the manuscript, fully formatted, back to you to add the correct page numbers to the index listings.

As the editor of the book, you will have to check the final galley to see that no errors have been made in the reformatting or printing of the book. This is very important, as I once found that several pages were missing from one of my books. Someone who wasn't intimately familiar with the text might not notice that. It is imperative that you get the author to look over and approve the galley, too, because changes may have been made that she has not agreed to. And once the book is printed it is very expensive to make corrections. Depending on how serious the errors were, the entire print run might have to be thrown out.

## HOW AND WHEN TO QUESTION AN AUTHOR

How and when to ask an author about his manuscript is a very important matter in editing. An editor often needs to discuss her edits with the author as the style the author uses may not be correct or according to preferred styles of the type of publication he is writing for. An author may prefer to emphasize some of his points by inappropriately capitalizing certain words, putting them in all caps, or underlining them. He may sprinkle his writing with many exclamation points. Before an editor changes the author's style, she needs to explain her reasons. Sometimes the author wants his manuscript exactly the way he has written and punctuated it and it would be wise if the editor found that out before she has made changes to the whole manuscript.

The editor need not write long notes on the pages explaining every change she has made. This could add greatly to the time it takes to edit the manuscript, and most authors appreciate the corrections of spelling, repeated words, and punctuation. Good editing always makes an author's manuscript much better and certainly more professional looking. Short notes can be written in the margins, if necessary. A list of notes on a separate sheet of paper, indicating the page and line they refer to can be composed at any time during the editing process. Often, an editor wants to explain her edits and deletions to the author so that the author can understand the reasoning behind them. This is especially true when the suggested changes refer to the story or theme of the piece. Sometimes whole sentences need to be rewritten to make them clearer. There is always the possibility of the editor misunderstanding what the author intended and it must be discussed. Always the author should look at the entire manuscript one last time before it goes to the printer.

Authors can be sensitive about and protective of their written creations so editors need to be careful not to appear overly critical or demeaning in any way. When an editor must make a lot of changes in a manuscript, she should explain why without insulting the author's intelligence. Editors should consider themselves in partnership with the author in making the writing the best it can be.

The relationship between author and editor can be emotional, and although I never lie to an author, I do critique as gently as I can. When I need to make a negative comment about something my client wrote, I first praise the writing in general, often pointing out certain passages I thought were excellent. Then I say something like, "I didn't understand what you meant in the last sentence of the first paragraph. Would you explain it to me?" I have found that as the author tries to explain it, he often makes the necessary changes himself because he can see it more clearly. If it was a novel I was editing I might say, "It would seem that your protagonist was stepping out of character in the third chapter. Was there a reason for this?" I never tell an author how to write, but I do ask questions, and if he seems to be going off in the wrong direction I try to gently lead him back onto the right path.

An editor should never argue with an author. When an author bristles at the changes I have made in his manuscript, I state my reasons for the edits and let the author decide whether to accept them or not. Even if I strongly disagree with him, I say, "It's your book and your money and it is your decision, not mine. I'm simply making suggestions based on my training and experience as an editor." After I have said that, the author almost always accepts the changes and the conflict is over. After all, when the author is paying the editor to work on his book, he wants the editor to be honest with him. He knows he needs the editor's professional services—and advice. Otherwise he would not have hired her.

## OFFERING GUIDANCE

When working with a new writer whose work is not yet ready for me to edit, I make suggestions as to how to organize their book. Often it helps if an author makes an outline of the book before beginning to rewrite it. It can serve as a compass and provide a checklist of what they need to do to write a book that will appeal to their target reader. The following are some basic guidelines I provide to authors to help them organize their work.

- Choose a descriptive title. At this point consider it simply a working title. You can add a subtitle that tells more about the book. Then try to sum up your book in one short sentence. This serves to help you clarify what your book is about and better focus on the subject-matter.
- Write a brief summary of the book. It will help you get to the essence of the information contained in your book. Think of how you would describe your book to others. Explain the purpose of your book and what it will do for the reader: enlighten, educate, or entertain. Tell how your book opens, what it is about, and how it ends. Include some of the highlights, specific events, dialogue, or interesting facts.
- Write an outline or a table of contents with chapter titles. Under each chapter title write a paragraph or two explaining what it is about. This can help you determine the order in which you will present your information. By preparing an outline of your book, you will be able to keep on track as you write.

Ask the author if he would like to schedule another meeting with you after he has organized his material. It's best for the author to send his new outline to you before the meeting so that you can read what he has done and make suggestions when you meet for a consultation. Be sure to make notes as you read it so that you can be sure that you are addressing each item. Begin with praise for the improvement and be specific. Make positive suggestions and avoid criticism. Here is your opportunity to help the author build on his strengths. An editor, especially one who works directly with an author who does not have a publisher involved, must be more than a person who makes sure the manuscript meets all the criteria of a professional document. She must also be a bit of a magician who brings out the best in an author, who discovers the author's inner fire and talents, and transforms the author's words into a work of art. Too much to ask! you might say, but a first-rate editor is like an excellent teacher who cares about her students and wants them to be the best they can be.

## A RELATIONSHIP OF CONFIDENCE

Editors are often called book doctors and I can understand why. We try to bring the written work to optimum health. There should be some kind of creed for editors similar to the Hippocratic Oath a physician takes. There are two things that I believe an editor should swear to.

- The first is to do no harm. An editor should set aside his own judgment about how something should be written. His job is to enhance what has been written by helping to make it clearer and to apply the rules of writing without changing the author's "voice" or the meaning, emotional impact, or artistry of the piece. An editor must not infuse the author's work with her own biases, beliefs, or writing style.
- The second is to consider every literary composition he works with confidential. The editor should not divulge the concept, subject, or any other facet of the written work to others without the author's express consent. The editor should also keep his opinion of the author's character, ability, and intelli-

gence to himself. The relationship between the author and the editor must be one of respect and trust.

The following is an excerpt from the Oath of Hippocrates that expresses the need for confidentiality:

> "Whatever, in connection with my professional practice . . . I see or hear, in the life of men, which ought not to be spoken of abroad, I will not divulge, as reckoning that all such should be kept secret."

An editor who is dedicated to her profession will encourage the author every step of the way and nurture the writing as though it were her own work. And, since we have chosen this noble profession of editing, I don't think that is too much to ask of ourselves.

## A Relationship of Professionalism

One last thing about the author/editor relationship. Remember at all times that this is a professional relationship. It is tempting at times to discuss personal matters with your client but it is not wise during the time that you are working with the client, whether of the same sex or of the opposite sex. If you were to forge an intimate friendship with your client or become involved romantically it would change the dynamics of the relationship. You would no longer have the objectivity to work together in the same way. Just as a physician should not become personally involved with his patient, nor an employer with her employee, nor an attorney with his client, an editor should not become personally involved with her author/client. It is unethical for many reasons. A physician, employer, attorney, editor and others in a position of authority must be responsible for keeping the relationship on a professional level.

You can be friendly with your clients and even occasionally get together away from work in a group setting such as a party at their home. Many of my clients have become friends but while I was working with them I kept the relationship more formal. This policy is not only best for the client, it is best for the editor as well. For example, on rare occasions I have accepted a dinner invitation with a client and his or her spouse, but I was unable to relax and enjoy an evening of friendly casual conversation. Inevitably, the client turned it into a discussion of her book and I felt like I was working. For me, it was more like a consultation.

I don't enjoy lunch or dinner meetings because I don't feel that I can direct my full attention either to the meal or to the business at hand. I was taught not to talk with my mouth full. So, not only am I not enjoying the meal, I'm not doing a very good job of consulting either.

So how do you keep your editor/client relationship professional? Here are some suggestions.

## Do:

- Let your clients know that you appreciate their paying your invoice promptly (if they do).
- Praise them for their writing talents and/or improving their writing (but only if it's true).
- Try always to be direct and honest in your evaluation of various facets of their writing without being disparaging. Remember, your opinion is what they are paying you for.
- Limit your discussion of your private life to such things as your hobbies, favorite restaurants, former employment, place of birth, etc., nothing too personal or revealing.
- Keep your face-to-face meetings in your or your client's office (can include home office), if possible. Otherwise, suggest meeting in a public place such as a library or coffee shop.
- Limit phone calls to your client to regular office hours whenever possible and encourage your clients to do the same. Explain that you don't work on weekends.
- Ask about your clients' background or personal history only as it applies to the manuscript they are writing.

- Change the subject if they begin to delve too deeply into your private life.

## Don't:

- Don't discuss politics or religion unless you know that you both feel exactly the same way about them.
- Don't tell clients their book is destined to be a bestseller. No one can know that.
- Don't complain about any of your other clients or reveal anything about their personal lives.
- Don't gossip about or demean a mutual acquaintance.
- Don't tell them your troubles, particularly not on their time, which they are paying you for.

When I first began I did not meet prospective clients in my home if they were strangers, as most of them were, in the beginning. I would meet them in a coffee shop or at the public library. If you live alone or are home alone most of the day, you may wish to do something like that. Now if I will be meeting a new client in person I check them out as much as I can. Because I work mainly by referral, I usually know the person who recommended me to the writer and I call and ask him or her about the person. Then, when we do meet at my home, the person who referred the writer knows that the client will be here that day and that provides me with a certain amount of security. I have never had any problems but I maintain a thoroughly professional demeanor.

Although I am always courteous I don't engage in deeply personal discussions. Your attitude with your client has a great deal to do with the way you are treated. It is preferable to develop a relationship of mutual respect with your clients than to develop a close friendship with them. By the same token, I don't often edit for friends (even the ones who intend to pay me) because I feel it is important to maintain our friendship and I am afraid that I can't be totally objective with a friend's manuscript. I am too concerned about their feelings to tell them any-thing negative about their work.

## A WORD OF CAUTION

Sometimes acquaintances will ask me to read their manuscript and tell them what I think of it. Some even tell me that their book is so good that they know I will enjoy it. When it becomes apparent that what they want is a reading and critique from a professional editor without being charged for it, I suggest that we schedule a consultation so that we can discuss it and I can give them an estimate of my charges. As reading a 200- or 300-page manuscript would take many hours of my time, I don't even do it for my friends. I have several books on my nightstand that I really want to read but just haven't gotten around to yet.

I find it hard to understand why anyone would ask an editor for free professional services. If they had a friend who was a doctor, would they ask him to give them a free physical exam and diagnosis?

Other freelance editors have had similar requests. One of them told me about an experience she had when she read her friend's book, as a favor, and critiqued it. Not only was the friend ungrateful for the time she spent on it, he was insulted when the editor told him it needed work. Apparently, he wanted her stamp of approval, not her honest professional opinion. The incident ended up destroying their friendship.

When people pay for a product or a service, they value it a lot more. When they pay nothing, they are less likely to appreciate its worth.

# 🙖6🙔

## *Styles and Usage*

What follows are some of the basic things you must know to become a book editor—or even a proofreader. Some of the most common errors writers make are included here. Also discussed are some of the errors that are most commonly overlooked by editors, usually because they aren't obvious. Some are difficult to see, such as two spaces between words and two spaces after a period and before the next sentence.

Those who grew up with typewriters were used to spacing twice between sentences. And they often continued that practice when using a word program on a computer. With most typewriters the extra space was needed to better indicate the ends and beginnings of sentences. With the computer's proportional letters and automatic justification, however, that is no longer necessary.

## STYLES

What are styles? In manuscript editing, style refers to rules related to capitalization, spelling, hyphenation, and abbreviations; punctuation including ellipsis points, parentheses, and quotation marks; and the way numbers are treated.

A style sheet is a record of terms kept by a manuscript editor to document particular usages for a specific manuscript. For example, the spelling of a name could be spelled a number of different ways, such as *Stephen, Stephan,* and *Steven.* Spelling is tricky because, in addition to names, the same word can often be correctly spelled two or more different ways, such as *analogue* and *analog, dialog* and *dialogue, catalog* and *catalogue, indexes* and *indices, appendixes* and *appendices.*

When an editor sees a word that she knows is not misspelled, she might not notice that it was spelled differently in another part of the book. Things like that are hard to remember, so making notes in a style sheet will help an editor to quickly check them—and remind her to look for them.

Although it is often not possible, it is helpful to read the entire manuscript through before beginning to edit it. Then you can start making notes in your style sheet that will help you in your editing later.

If I am working with a manuscript that has a lot of characters, such as a novel or family history, I write down the names of each one as I encounter him or her. I note their relationship to the other characters, their age, and any other identifying information that I think might be important later on. Since it is hard to recall so many details, I can refer to my notes whenever I encounter that character again to see if there is any discrepancy or inconsistency that needs to be corrected.

## PUNCTUATION (AMERICAN STYLE)

### Quotation marks

When do you use double quotation marks (") and when do you use single quotation marks (')? If you will be using only one set of quotation marks, make them double, never (or rarely) single. The rule is this: quoted words, phrases, and sentences are enclosed in double quotation marks. Quotations within quotations are enclosed in single quotation marks. When you have a quotation within a quotation that is within yet another quotation, that third set is enclosed in double quotation marks. The following is an excellent example from *The Chicago Manual of Style, 16th Edition.*

> "Don't be absurd!" said Henry. "To say that 'I mean what I say' is the same as 'I say what I mean' is to be as confused as Alice at the Mad Hatter's tea party. You remember what the Hatter said to her: 'Not the same thing a bit! Why you might just as well say that "I see what I eat" is the same thing as "I eat what I see"!'"

Notice the absence of commas in the above as well as the placement of the exclamation point. The comma is not used in the above example because it is not necessary in this context. Normally you would use a comma before a quotation as in "He said, 'I do believe you are right.'"

Regarding the exclamation point, it is placed after the third set of double quotations and before the second set (single quotes) which is the Hatter speaking. The concluding set of double quotation marks belongs to Henry's speech.

For more detailed explanations of the use of punctuation and for some exceptions to the rules, refer to the *Chicago Manual.* I can only touch on some of the more common errors I have seen in my years of editing.

## Periods with quotation marks

When a sentence is enclosed in quotation marks, the period ending the sentence is placed inside the closing quotation mark. If the quoted sentence is included within another sentence, the period at the end of it is omitted or replaced by a comma unless it comes at the end of the including sentence. In that case, a single period serves both sentences and is placed inside the closing quotation mark.

## Periods with parentheses or brackets

When an independent sentence is enclosed in parentheses or brackets the period belongs inside. When the enclosed matter comes at the end of an including sentence, the period should be placed outside the parentheses or brackets.

## Exclamation points

These should be used sparingly. Otherwise, they lose their impact. If the sentence itself is obviously emphatic, an exclamation point is simply redundant. In good, clear, expressive writing exclamation points are rarely necessary. And more than one exclamation point at the end of a sentence is an absolute no-no.

## Commas

The comma indicates the smallest break in sentence structure. It usually denotes a slight pause. The use of commas in a series has changed over the years. We once were taught that no comma was necessary between the last two elements of a series. But now the rule is, when a comma joins the last two elements in series of three or more, a comma goes before the conjunction. For example it's *Tom, Dick, and Harry,* not *Tom, Dick and Harry.*

Most writers use far too many commas. If it helps clarify a sentence a comma should be used. If there is no good reason for it and it interrupts continuity it should not be used.

## Semicolons

A semicolon is most commonly used between two independent clauses not joined by a conjunction to signal a closer connection between them than a period would. Semicolons are used less often than they were in the past. Generally, use a period when the sentence expresses two complete thoughts, not a semicolon: *She thought she was perfect. She certainly wasn't.*

When items in a sentence involve internal punctuation, they should be separated by semicolons for the sake of clarity. Example: *She had three children. They were Alice, 4; Tommy, 6; and Nathan, 12.*

The semicolon should be placed outside quotation marks or parentheses: *He said, "I'll be there"; he never intended to come.*

My preference in nearly all cases is to use a period instead of a semicolon when each phrase can be a complete sentence. Generally, it gives each thought more emphasis. It is more contemporary usage, too. Example: *He said he'd be there. He didn't show up, though.*

### Question marks

A question mark is used to mark a query to express doubt: *Who are you?*

A question mark should be used at the end of a directly interrogative element that is part of a sentence: *Who was that man? she wondered.*

The question mark should be placed inside the quotation marks, parentheses, or brackets only when it is part of the quoted or parenthetical matter: *Was he lying when he said, "I am the police"?*

### Colons

Colons are used to introduce a speech in dialogue.
*ANNA: I thought you'd never get here.*

A colon is also used to introduce a list or a series and it should follow a speaker's introductory remark. It should be place outside quotation marks or parentheses: *He had only one thing to say about "The Tempest": it was too long.*

STARTING YOUR CAREER AS A FREELANCE EDITOR

## Hyphens and Dashes

Hyphens and dashes all have specific appearances and uses. A hyphen is
the shortest; an en dash is slightly longer, and an em dash is about the
length of two en dashes. There is also the 2-em dash which is about
the length of two em dashes joined together, and a 3-em dash about
the length of three em dashes. All are unbroken lines. Although many
readers may not notice the difference between a hyphen and an en
dash, the correct use of it is an indication of editorial precision. This is
a case in which an editor has to have a particularly sharp eye. The following are examples of these symbols.

hyphen -
en dash –
em dash —
2-em dash ——
3-em dash ———

**Hyphens** are used in compound words and names and in word
division. They can help clarify a phrase: a small animal hospital (the
hospital is small); a small-animal hospital (the animal is small). They can
also be used as separators, as in telephone numbers: 1-800-555-1212;
and can appear in email addresses: literaryarts-ca.org. Hyphens are used
for end-of-the line word breaks where the hyphen divides the word by
syllables: *metro-nome*. They are used for compound terms: *a full-length
gown, an eight-by-ten-foot room, an eleven-year-old boy.*

**En Dashes.** The principal use of the en dash is to connect num-
bers and, sometimes, words. It can stand for "to":
*The years 2000–2005 were spent in college.*
*The show airs Sunday, 1:30–2:00 on CBS.*
*The Chicago–New York train leaves at 7:30 AM.*
An en dash may also be used to indicate a number range that is
ongoing: *The book was written by Jane Doe (1955–).*

**Em dashes,** the most frequently used and most versatile of the dashes, are used instead of commas, parentheses, or colons. A common error is spacing before or after an em dash. There should be no space.

An em dash can indicate a sudden break in thought: *"Would he—do you think—really come to my party?"*

An em dash is often used instead of parentheses: *They all attended—Tom, Dick, and Harry—and all brought presents.*

It can indicate an interruption in thought: *"Well, I thought I would be going with—"*

**2-Em Dashes** represent a missing word or part of a word. When a whole word is missing there is a space before and after the dash. When only part of a word is missing no space appears between the dash and the existing part of the word. A 2-em dash can be used to disguise an expletive: *He made the same f____g mistake again!*

**3-Em Dashes,** followed by a period, are used in a bibliography to represent the same author or editor named in the preceding entry:

Smithson, Vince D. *Nature's Medicine.* Atlanta: University Press, 1979.

_____. *Herbs that Heal.* Atlanta: University Press, 1985.

## GRAMMAR AND PARTS OF SPEECH

We all studied this in school but it's hard to remember all of the rules and definitions of the various parts of speech. And knowing the traditional terminology can help you as an editor explain why you made the edits you did. Huge volumes have been written about grammar and this subject could easily take up a whole book but you'll be happy to know that I am going to try to make this as brief and simple as possible, touching only on the major points.

Grammar is defined as the rules governing how words are put together in a sentence. These rules govern most constructions. The few constructions that are not covered by these rules are idioms and usage.

Rules, though, are meant to be broken and in modern American English, these rules are broken all the time. Still, it will make you appear more knowledgeable if you adhere to most of them, unless they get in the way too much.

Grammar focuses on parts of speech and their syntax, which is the study of the patterns of formation of sentences and phrases from words. Words are classified according to their functions in sentences. It is generally agreed that there are eight parts of speech: nouns, pronouns, verbs, adjectives, adverbs, prepositions, conjunctions, and interjections. However, some modern grammarians insist that there are as few as three and others believe that there are "about fifteen." For my purposes here, I'm going with the traditional school of thought.

In addition to the eight parts of speech, there are also **articles**. The **definite article** is *the. The* specifies something or someone in particular, especially if there is only one of them: *The world is round. The Dodgers won.* The **indefinite articles** are *a* and *an. A* is used before words beginning with a consonant sound, and *an* is used before a vowel sound: *A rose was blooming in the garden. An iris can be many different colors.*

## Nouns

A **noun** is a word that denotes a thing, place, person, quality, state, or action. It functions in a sentence as the subject or object of an action expressed by a verb. It can also be the object of a preposition. There are proper nouns and common nouns. Proper nouns denote individuals and personifications and are always capitalized: *the Pacific Ocean; the coastline of Southern California.* The word *coastline* is a common noun but the word *Southern* becomes a proper noun in this sentence because it is part of the accepted title of the region. If we were to say *the southern tip of California* it would be considered a common noun.

A general name common to all persons, places, or things is called a common noun. In modern English, common nouns are not capitalized: *the sea; the sky.*

There are **concrete** and **abstract nouns.** Anything physical that can be perceived by the senses is a concrete noun: *Some books are to be tasted, others to be swallowed* [Francis Bacon]. An abstract noun is a quality, action, or idea which cannot be perceived by the senses: *A foolish consistency is the hobgoblin of little minds* [Ralph Waldo Emerson].

There are also collective nouns, which name a group of individuals as though they were one: *jury, committee, family, flock, regiment.* And, depending on the purpose it serves, a collective noun can be either singular or plural. In the sentence, *The family was united in its decision,* meaning it acted as one person, *family* is a singular form of the collective noun. In *The family were arguing over where to go on vacation,* the family members were acting as individuals, so in this case the *family* is considered a plural noun.

## Pronouns

A **pronoun** is an identifying word which substitutes for a noun or, sometimes, another pronoun. A pronoun can indicate a noun (such as a person's name) already mentioned to avoid repetition: *Charlie* (noun) is head of the department; *he* (pronoun) makes all the decisions. There are several kinds of pronouns: personal, demonstrative, indefinite, relative, interrogative, numerical, reflexive, and reciprocal.

A **personal pronoun** indicates the speaker, the person spoken to, or the person, place, or thing spoken about. The speaker is first person: *I, my or mine, me, we, our or ours, us.* The person spoken to is second person: *you, your, yours.* The person, place, or thing spoken about is third person: *he, she, it, they, his, her, hers, him, her, its, their, theirs, them.* Here is a sentence that contains all three forms of personal pronouns: *I loaned you my watch but you gave it to him and he lost it.*

**Demonstrative pronouns** are *this, that, these,* and *those.* They indicate a person or thing specifically: *This is my coat. That coat is yours. These are my crayons. Those colored pencils are yours.*

**Indefinite pronouns** refer to people or things in general. Some indefinite pronouns are: *all, everybody, everything, anyone, another, many,* *more, several, either, neither, both, each*. An example of usage in a sentence is *Anyone can make a mistake. Everybody knows that.*

A **relative pronoun** plays two roles, both as a pronoun and as a connective. It is a subject or object in a subordinate part of a sentence, and it joins the subordinate to a more important part of a sentence. Relative pronouns are *who, which, that, what, whose, and whom.* Example: *Which one is the girl who fell down the rabbit hole?* Some compound relative pronouns are *whoever, whosoever, whatever, whichever, whatsoever,* and *whomever.* Example: *Whoever told you that was mistaken.*

An **interrogative pronoun** helps ask a question. They are *who, which, what, whom,* and *whose.* Examples: *Whose bracelet is that? Which one of you found it? What shall we do with it?*

**Reflexive pronouns** are formed by adding *self* or *selves* to the personal pronoun. They are *myself, yourself, himself, herself, itself, ourselves, yourselves,* and *themselves.* This kind of pronoun can be used as an object referring to the same person as the subject: *She travels by herself.*

A **reciprocal pronoun** represents two or more people or things interchanging the action of the verb: *They have always taken care of each other.*

### Verbs

**Verbs** express an action, state of being, occurrence, or relation between two things. **Inflection** or **conjugation** of a verb involves changes of form according to person and number, tense, voice (active and passive), and mood.

**Person and number** refer to who and how many performed the action.

**Tense** indicates the action performed. Present tense, for example, would be *know;* past tense would be *knew;* past participle would be *known. I know the boy. I knew the boy. I have known the boy for a long time.*

**Voice** indicates whether the subject of the verb performed (active) or received (passive) the action: *Alice rode her bike* (active). *The bike was ridden by Alice* (passive).

**Mood** indicates the frame of mind of the performer. Verbs have three moods: the indicative, which expresses actuality: *I dance*; the subjunctive which expresses contingency: *I might dance*; and the imperative: which expresses a command: *Dance!* Other examples of the use of a subjunctive include sentences with conditional clauses contrary to fact: *If I were young again, I'd do things differently*; and subordinate clauses after verbs like *wish*: *Oh, I wish I were in the land of cotton.*

## Adverbs

**Adverbs** modify verbs, adjectives, or other adverbs or adverbial phrases, clauses, and sentences, and alter their meaning in some way. For example, in the sentence *He walks slowly,* the adverb *slowly* modifies the verb *walks.* In *He walks with a very slow gait,* the adverb *very* modifies the adjective *slow.* In *She moves very slowly,* the adverb *very* modifies the adverb *slowly.* Adverbs may indicate place or direction *(where, there),* time *(today, tomorrow),* degree *(nearly, completely),* manner *(carefully, slowly),* belief or doubt *(surely, maybe),* and how often *(never, always).*

Adverbs are classified as simple or conjunctive depending on their use. A simple adverb alters the meaning of a single word. A conjunctive adverb modifies the sentence or clause it appears in.

## Adjectives

An adjective modifies a noun or pronoun by limiting, qualifying, or describing it in one of three forms of degree: positive *(happy, beautiful)*, comparative *(happier, more beautiful)*, or superlative *(happiest, most beautiful)*. Adjectives are distinguished by having endings like *-er* and *-est*, as in *bigger, biggest.* An adjective usually precedes the noun it directly modifies: *prettiest* dress, *heavier* truck.

## Prepositions

A preposition is a word that combines with a noun or pronoun to form a phrase. It expresses the relationship between words: *from* here *to* there;

one *after* another; water *under* the bridge. Examples of prepositions are *to, through, in, into, for, on, at, with, about, along, after, before, during, between, among,* and *from.* In casual speech, it's no longer a crime to end a sentence with a preposition. It's now perfectly all right to say, *That's where she came from; He's the man she gave her heart to; They're the couple everybody is talking about.*

## Conjunctions

Conjunctions, such as *and, or, but, though, if, unless, however,* and *because* connect sentences, clauses, phrases, or words. There are two kinds of conjunctions: coordinate and subordinate. Coordinate conjunctions join words, independent clauses, or parts of a sentence that are of the same rank or order: *Virtue is bold and goodness never fearful* [Shakespeare]. Examples of these are *and, but, or, yet;* conjunctive adverbs *however, nevertheless;* and correlative conjunctions *neither/nor.* Subordinate conjunctions introduce subordinate clauses. *Where, when, after, while, if, unless, since, because, although,* and *whether* are subordinate conjunctions: *I will go when I am ready. He won't stay unless he's invited to dinner.* Subordinate conjunctions may also function as prepositions.

It is no longer considered wrong to begin a sentence with a conjunction. And I do that frequently.

## Interjections

Interjections are usually used to express an emotional reaction: *Oh! Ow! Yipes! Hurrah!* They are also used for emphasis: *Aha!* The interjection has no grammatical relation to the other parts of the sentence.

There are a few other principles of word usage that are worthy of consideration, such as the following.

- In most cases, use the active rather than the passive voice: *I'd love for you to come to my party,* not *Your presence is requested.*

- Write clearly. Simplifying your writing is not dumbing it down. It is making it available to readers who don't want to struggle with trying to figure out what you mean. According to Walter Savage Landor, "Clear writers, like fountains, do not seem so deep as they are; the turbid look the most profound."

- Be concise. Long sentences and strings of polysyllabic words tend to muddy your meaning. Sprinkling a lot of arcane words throughout your writing also makes it difficult to read and understand for those with less than genius IQ. Not all authors agree with this principle. William Faulkner said of Ernest Hemingway, "He has never been known to use a word that might send a reader to the dictionary." Hemingway responded, "Poor Faulkner. Does he really think big emotions come from big words?"

- Get rid of unnecessary words and avoid redundancies. Superfluous words are everywhere, on broadcast news, in newspapers and magazines, in movies and television. It's hard to understand why anyone needs to say *enter into an agreement*. You can't enter *out* of anything. And why say *dropped down* as though it were possible to drop *up?* Cops never make that mistake. It's much quicker to say, "Drop the gun!" Time is of the essence. There are so many other redundancies littering our language: *revert back, reiterate again, previous history,* and *follow behind*. If a word doesn't add information, why use it?

Because language is in a constant state of flux, common usage alters the meaning and proper usage of a word. So-called correct word usage is a temporary thing. When a word is so frequently misused that its meaning changes, its new usage becomes standard. Thus, it is no longer wrong. The words "nerd" and "geek" were once derogatory terms, meaning people who were stupid and unattractive. Now, though, when those words are coupled with the word "computer," as in "computer nerds" or "computer geeks," they aren't so derogatory. There is a company called the Geek Squad and they are highly admired experts who can come to your home or office and help you with your computer or just about any other technological equipment. The Geeks certainly are not stupid and when they get your computer running like silk again, they aren't unattractive; they suddenly look like Prince Charming. And we all know about computer nerds who are so brilliant and innovative that they are much admired, too. Some of them are also billionaires. And success is beautiful.

We often think of a dictionary as an authority, but it doesn't dictate proper word usage. It is merely a guide to the current standard in word definitions. And, have you noticed, all dictionaries don't agree with each other regarding definitions?

## MISSPELLINGS

An editor has to be a very good speller in order to notice when a word is misspelled. Or is *not* a good speller and knows it, so when she is in doubt, she looks it up. I believe I am the latter. Among my spelling challenges is remembering which words are spelled with an "ie" (like *piece*) and which are spelled with an "ei," (like *seize*). There are some rules, but there are exceptions to almost all rules, so knowing them might not help anyway. The little poem that is meant to help you remember this rule goes like this:

I before E
except after C,
or when sounded as A,
as in *neighbor* and *weigh*.

I wrote about this rule in my book *The Birds and Bees of Words*. I found that there are many other exceptions to the "ie" versus "ei" spelling. And there are words that don't fit either of the above rules. They have *E* before *I* for no reason at all. It's enough to make an editor crazy. Here are just a few of these words: *either, neither, feisty, forfeit, heifer, height, leisure, seize, seizure, sleight, seismology,* and *weird* (and there are more).

You can't rhyme them based on their spelling. So don't expect a thorough knowledge of phonetics to help you. It would seem that words like *height* and *weight* would rhyme—but *no! Height* rhymes with *white*, while *weight* rhymes with *hate*. The English language is such a mixture of so many different languages from all over the world, slang, profanity, technology, scientific terms, and so forth that phonetic spelling rarely applies. For example, *through, rough,* and *though* should rhyme because they all end in the letters *ough,* but they don't. *Through* is pronounced *throo, rough* is pronounced *ruff,* and *though* rhymes with *show, blow,* and *tow. How* and *now* should rhyme with *tow* but they don't. If one doesn't grow up using English, it has got to be extremely hard to learn the language. And if they learned it in England and then moved to America, they had to learn a lot of it all over again because British English and American English are so different from each other.

There is one spelling rule you can go by because there aren't many exceptions to it. The rule applies to the words ending in *cede, ceed,* and *sede,* which all rhyme with *seed.* All you have to know is that most of them end in *cede,* such as *concede, recede, accede, secede, intercede, retrocede,* and *precede.* Then you can easily memorize the exceptions because there are only four American English words of this group that do *not* end in *cede.* Three of them end in *ceed,* and they are *exceed, proceed,* and *succeed.* Only one word ends in *sede* and that one is *supersede.*

It's no wonder that words are so frequently misspelled. A person has to memorize the spelling of each one or spend a lot of time checking the dictionary for the word in question. A tall order, when the English language contains such an enormous number of words.

## BRITISH ENGLISH VERSUS AMERICAN ENGLISH

It's important to note the differences between British and American punctuation and spelling, and even definitions. When you are checking the spelling and punctuation of a document be sure that you understand who the readers are likely to be. Commas and periods are placed differently in British English documents. In American documents periods and commas nearly always go inside. In British documents they are placed according to the meaning of the sentence, which actually makes more sense. However, it is easier to remember the American rule than to analyze the sentence.

Many words are spelled differently. In many cases it is because Americans shortened or simplified the British spelling of the word, changing *neighbour* to *neighbor, flavour* to *flavor, travelled* to *traveled, manoeuvre* to *maneuver, oestrogen* to *estrogen,* and *paediatric* to *pediatric,* to name only a few. It would be difficult, I think, for an American to edit British writing and vice versa.

## MISUSED WORDS

Word confusion is another frequent error. These are words that are real words properly spelled but not the appropriate one for that particular sentence, such as *ravage* and *ravish. Ravage* means to wreak great destruction or devastation. *Ravish* means to abduct, rape, or carry away with emotion. Others that I have found frequently confused (or misspelled) are *plain* and *plane, staid* and *stayed, read* and *red,* as in "I red the book" and "The dress was read." Unless the dress had writing on it the word should have been *red.* Spell check won't catch those mistakes.

Perhaps the most commonly confused words are *affect* (to influence, to bring about a change) and *effect* (a result, a consequence). Other common errors are confusing *acclamation* (enthusiastic approval) with *acclimation* (adaptation to a climatic environment). Also *wreak,* pronounced *reek* (to inflict punishment on another, to avenge), which is often confused with *wreck,* pronounced *reck* (to destroy by collision). I hear this word frequently misused and mispronounced even on the news.

One of the words that bothers me is the common misuse of the word *notoriety,* when the person intends it to mean fame. *Notoriety* means shame, infamy, disrepute. *Fame* means a widespread reputation, as of a favorable character. I've even heard the word *notorious* used when the speaker meant *famous. Notorious* means widely and unfavorably known. *Famous* means renowned, celebrated. These are important distinctions.

Making notes of frequently confused words became almost a compulsion with me and I began writing down every one that I saw or heard until I had such a long list of them that I decided to write a book about them. Allworth Press published it in 2007. The title is *The Birds and Bees of Words: A Guide to the Most Common Errors in Usage, Spelling, and Grammar.* The book also contains chapters on word usage, old and new rules, word roots, new words and phrases, and frequently misspelled words. It can be used as a quick reference when you are editing.

And then there are words that are absolutes that people feel they must qualify even though it is wrong to do so. One such word is *unique.* Since *unique* means one of a kind, how can anything be *very unique? Perfect* is another one that is frequently qualified. *Perfect* describes an absolute, yes–or–no condition that cannot logically be said to exist in varying degrees. One can be *nearly* perfect but not the *most* perfect.

These and many other words, however, are constantly misused. And according to semanticists and lexicographers, their frequent and long-term misusage make them eventually acceptable. This is where an editor has a most difficult choice. She must decide whether to stick to the old rules which, in the above cases, make perfect sense if accuracy is important, or accept the new rules that have been created by sloppy writers (and speakers). I don't mean to demean anyone but that kind of usage just drives me up the wall.

When faced with the decision of whether or not to correct the misusage, consider the text in which it appears. If it is in formal writing, do correct it. Otherwise, discuss it with the author to see if he or she objects to your changes.

# 7

## *Editing Principles*

There are several stages of editing, whether a manuscript is being edited by an independent editor working directly for and with the author or is working in a publishing company and has been assigned the manuscript she will be editing.

The first thing to be considered is whether the manuscript is ready for editing. If it is not, then developmental editing must be done which directly shapes the content, the way it should be presented, how it should be handled and whether more documentation is needed. This kind of editing may involve a complete rewrite and a reorganization of the material. If an editor takes on a manuscript before it has been fully developed, it will have to be edited again after the changes have been made.

## COPYEDITING

Assuming the manuscript is ready and no reorganization needs to be done, the first stage is manuscript editing, also called copyediting or line editing. It is the most important and most time-consuming task. Attention must be paid to every detail in the manuscript, every word and mark of punctuation. It is edited for content, grammatical construction, spelling, clarity, and consistency. The editor may also be responsible for researching the spelling of foreign words, places, proper names, and scientific terminology, to name just a few.

The editor must have a thorough knowledge of the style to be followed. She must make decisions quickly and logically and be able to explain and defend them, if necessary. Publishing companies usually have at least four sets of experienced eyes who will each have a hand in the editing. For the freelance editor who has been hired by the author directly, she will be expected to handle all of the editing from first draft to completed manuscript. This is the reason that a freelance editor needs an extensive library of several kinds of stylebooks, dictionaries, encyclopedias, and special reference books relating to the manuscript she is editing. Her tasks also include what the *Chicago Manual* calls mechanical and substantive editing, which are described below.

## MECHANICAL EDITING

Mechanical editing includes seeing to it that a consistent style is followed in the text and in the documentation of tables and illustrations. Style refers to rules relating to capitalization, spelling, hyphenation, and abbreviations. It also includes punctuation such as commas, periods, semicolons, ellipsis points, parentheses, and quotation marks, as well as the way numbers are treated. The editor also must pay attention to grammar, syntax, and usage. The styles that must be applied to a manuscript are determined by book or journal publishers and by particular disciplines. Styles for trade books are different than styles for journals, periodicals, dissertations, scientific and medical writing, and so forth. The style of any work, as well as deviations from it, must be determined by the author, editor, and/or publisher before the process of editing begins.

## SUBSTANTIVE EDITING

The organization and presentation of the content of the manuscript is involved in the process of substantive editing. This is where the editor takes care of such remedial actions as reorganizing and tightening the text, improving the writing style, and clearing up ambiguities. It deals with the substance of the material. This type of editing should not be done by the editor without first discussing it with the publisher. If major substantive editing is necessary the author and/or publisher should be consulted, especially if it is a book-length work. The editor may wish to give the author a sample of the changes being considered before proceeding further.

## PROOFREADING

The final editing phase is proofreading. This is checking for typographical errors, word divisions (as in end-of-the line hyphenation), misplaced punctuation, wrong font, and sense. The proofreader also checks for extra spaces between words and sentences, misplaced or missing quotation marks, and other common errors such as more than one period at the end of a sentence or no period at all. This is done after all of the other editing has been completed.

## THE STAGES OF EDITING

In some cases, the same editor will perform all of the tasks. The "all-in-one" editor, which many freelance editors are, often go through the manuscript at least three times to do a thorough job.

The first stage, the initial editing, is the longest, as the editor will be closely examining the manuscript for the first time and trying to catch as many errors or problems as he can. At the end of the first stage, he will be able to determine if there is a logical beginning, middle, and end. He will have an image of the entire manuscript in his mind and be able to see weak spots in the story, continuity, and presentation.

The second time he goes through the manuscript he will be reviewing, refining, and correcting the editing. He will then turn it over to the author to review the changes he has made. Often the author will find some changes not to her liking and will request that some areas be put back the way she had them in the original.

That is where the third stage comes in, with the editor making some final edits to accommodate the wishes of the author. This stage can be difficult for a knowledgeable and seasoned editor because sometimes the author asks for things that are not up to professional standards. Then the editor has to decide whether to make changes that will please the author but weaken the manuscript, or to try to convince her that these changes are contraindicated and could make the work appear unprofessional.

This has happened a few times in my editing career. When it does, I explain to the author why I made the changes I did. Often, it is a matter of styles or taste. Sometimes it is just bad writing. For example, an author may want an exclamation point to follow every statement she wants to emphasize. Sometimes authors use several exclamation points together: !!! And that's really overkill. I have had a few manuscripts like that, and I will tell the client that the emotion was so clearly written that an exclamation point was not necessary; in fact, that it distracted from the mood of the piece.

Some authors underline and italicize words that they think are very important and want to call attention to. Sometimes they put the words in all caps. I believe in letting the reader decide for himself the magnitude of the material. These marks of emphasis are telling the reader what the author wants him to think and feel. I don't think readers want their emotional responses to be imposed upon by an author.

As I am an author, an editor, and an avid reader, I can see all three points of view. When I edit, I consider the reader's reaction, just as I do when I am writing my own books, articles, and other pieces aimed at the general reader. Somehow an editor needs to get it across to an author that what he or she writes must consider the reader first—before and instead of the author's own needs. If an author wishes to be published and to engage readers, he must write for his target audience. He must make his writing so strong and so clear that the reader gets it without the added embellishments and excess punctuation.

There may be times that an author does write only for himself and doesn't care whether what he has written is ever read by others. This is personal writing that one might do when keeping a diary or journal or writing poetry. I think most writers have probably started out that way. And all kinds of writing help one to become a better writer. When I have gone back and reread my journals of ten or twenty years ago, I can see that my writing has improved.

Not all manuscripts receive the services of all types and phases of editing, particularly in the case of a freelance editor who is the only one who sees the manuscript of an author. In a medium to large publishing company, many of the above tasks are done by different people. For example, an acquisitions editor or senior editor will usually be the first to see the manuscript. She will be the one to determine whether the potential book is for her company. If she thinks it is, she will pass it on to the CEO or Publisher of the company for final acceptance or rejection of the manuscript. Then it may go to the copyeditor, stylistic editor, and to the page designer and typesetter.

The type of editing you choose to do will depend on your abilities, training, and education. Specialization is mandatory since no one can edit all kinds of material and everyone has different levels of expertise. But no matter how good an editor you are, when you are working on a book you must have an excellent proofreader go through it before it goes to print.

As important as editing is, we can't overlook the importance of the final proofreading. Although authors are considered the primary proofreaders and they bear responsibility for any errors in the published work, a professional proofreader may be hired who can work with the author on this essential phase.

It is not just the text that has to be proofread. For books, the jacket and cover must also be proofed. The author's name, book title, publisher's imprint and any other matter that may be on the spine, front or back cover must be checked very carefully. Authors are considered the primary proofreaders and they bear responsibility for any errors in the published work. If the author doesn't feel qualified, a professional proofreader may be hired. Most indexes are prepared from the first set of proofs. However, editors usually proofread indexes.

For books, the jacket and cover must also be proofread. The author's name, book title, publisher's imprint and any other matter that may be on the spine, front or back cover must be checked very carefully.

## What the final proofing should include

The proofreader must read word for word against the edited manuscript and check all punctuation, paragraphs, capitalization, quotation marks, italics, etc. and be sure that any handwritten notes have been correctly included by the typesetter. To avoid any confusion between the final drafts, the proofreader must mark only the proofs, not the manuscript.

# 8

## *Methods of Editing*

No matter what method an editor uses, the first thing to be considered is how the editor keeps track of details in the manuscript as the editing progresses. As mentioned in a previous chapter, a style sheet helps the editor ensure consistency. As she goes through the manuscript, she makes notes that she can refer to later. The style sheet should contain an alphabetical list of words or terms to be capitalized, italicized, spelled, or in some other way treated in the same way throughout the document. Notes about characters and their relationship to other characters are also helpful. They will be easier to find if you put the page number by the entry each time it appears.

I learned this the hard way. When I hadn't made notes from the beginning, I would have to go back through the manuscript and look for the inconsistencies—which are not so easy to find. It is also time-consuming. Now I start making notes with the first read-through.

### FACT CHECKING

Although the author is finally responsible for the accuracy of the work, a good editor will also look for obvious errors such as mathematical calculations, bibliographic references, and geographic locations. These errors should be pointed out to the author or, if the editor simply suspects it is an error, she may be able to quickly check the math herself or look up some of the facts in reference books. She should make notes of these as well so that she can put them into a memo to the author as she goes along. The editor's comments and questions should be concise and ask for clarification or verification.

## EDITING ON PAPER

At the beginning of the author/editor relationship the decision must be made as to how the manuscript will be presented. Some authors will want to give you a printed copy of their manuscript and ask you to mark your edits on it in pen or pencil. If they wish to work that way, you need to explain that it must be double spaced and contain at least one-inch margins to accommodate the editor's notes. Even when I am editing on paper I ask for a CD of the manuscript or to have the file sent to me electronically. I never transcribe from an audio recording or type a computer version of a manuscript that has been created on a typewriter. I suggest the author find a typist/transcriber to do that work.

When I edit directly on the printed page I mark the changes and corrections in red ink so that they can readily be seen by the author. Pencil markings are hard to read. Some editors use proofreaders marks but, because most of their clients don't understand them, they are rarely used anymore, except inside a publishing company where everyone who will be working on the manuscript is familiar with them.

The edited manuscript must be photocopied for the editor's files and the original pages mailed or given to the author. The author can decide whether he wants to accept the changes recommended, and mark any changes he wants to make. I ask authors to photocopy the paper manuscripts with their handwritten comments to send back to me. Since any manuscript edited in this way is one of a kind, the work would have to be done over if the manuscript got lost. Usually, every page does not contain notes and comments so I ask my clients to send back only the pages that have handwritten notes on them.

Occasionally, when the author has approved of the edits, he may wish to type in the changes himself. That saves me the time involved in typing them and, of course, saves the client money. Often the author is on a tight budget and I am happy to help him learn how to do as much as he can himself. My clients appreciate my thoughtfulness and are more likely to recommend my services to other writers. He will then copy the manuscript onto a compact disk and mail it back to me or send it electronically over the Internet as an attachment to an email. When we both have agreed on all the changes, I proof the final draft, make any final corrections if necessary, and send the electronic file back to the author.

## MAKING THE EDITS ON THE COMPUTER

Sometimes editors make their changes directly on the author's electronic file. In some cases you may have to convert the file and reformat it to make it ready to edit, usually in a word-processing program. When you are working on an electronic file, you should be very familiar with the software. Many word-processing programs have become powerful text editors. If you don't already know them, you will have to learn how to use search and replace options, which can save many steps. Use the software's "help" documentation. It will explain in detail how to indicate and track your edits, as well as many other processes that can be immensely helpful in your editing.

For book-length works which may arrive with each chapter in a separate file, you will have to assemble the text into a single electronic file. Doing this at the beginning will save you a great deal of time. At this point you can also delete extra spaces, such as two or more consecutive spaces between sentences. Many authors indent using the space bar instead of creating first-line paragraph indents. These should be changed using tabs or software-defined indents so that they are consistent. Replace words that have been underlined when they should be in italics, such as titles of books, movies, newspapers, magazines, etc. These rules can be found in the *Chicago Manual*. Fix quotation marks and apostrophes as well as commas and periods relative to quotation marks. Adjust line spacing, fonts, and margins. Making these adjustments and corrections at the beginning will make your editing go faster and will likely help in maintaining the consistency of these types of edits.

You can make changes in the document by inserting, deleting, or moving text or graphics. The edits you do on the computer can be tracked using the "track changes" option in Microsoft Word, so that the author can readily see what you have done. He can then accept or reject the changes. Both the editor and the author will have to understand how to use this tool for it to work for them. In Word 2010 more than one person can work on a document at the same time. This may or may not work for you as the editor.

Once the author is comfortable with the editing that is being done, he may ask the editor to simply make the changes herself on the electronic manuscript and send it back to him for final approval. This method is the fastest and usually the most accurate because the author doesn't have to be concerned that he might make new mistakes and not be aware of them.

The downside of this, to the author, is that he may not recall what his original version was so he can't compare the edits to what he wrote. Once authors trust me, though, they are no longer concerned. They realize that the more times the manuscript goes back and forth, the more time it takes to finish it. And the more of my time he'll have to pay for.

## THE MECHANICS OF EDITING

*The Chicago Manual of Style* describes the mechanics of editorial marking very clearly, showing how insertions and deletions are indicated, as well as transpositions (changing the order of letters, words, or phrases), punctuation, and other corrections that need to be made. It covers the mechanics of editing on paper as well as the mechanics of electronic editing. Whether you are just beginning your career as an editor or have been editing for many years, it would be beneficial for you to read those sections of *Chicago* to refresh your memory and to learn new things. Whether you are an expert or not, you can never know everything there is to know about editing, just as no one can ever know all there is to know about writing. With each manuscript I edit I learn something new.

Whether you are editing on paper or electronically, you should make a copy of the author's original unedited copy and save separate copies of each significant version as you go along. I find that the best way to keep track of the versions is to date them. That way there is no doubt as to which copy is the most recent. It is also very important to save open documents frequently so that everything you have done to that point is preserved. There are few things as distressing as having the electricity go off after you have been working for hours on a project and lose all the changes because the document was not saved during that time. And, just in case my computer crashes, I copy the manuscript to a CD or flash drive at least once a week. I can't charge for the hours I worked on a manuscript if that version disappeared and I had to do all the work over. That has happened to me. In the course of twenty years of editing, just about every bad thing has happened at least once. That kind of learning is called the school of hard knocks. Far better to avoid the possible mistakes in the present than to have to pay for them in the future.

As I often work with authors over a period of weeks or even months, I send the author the latest version of the manuscript, as far as I've gotten, once a month along with my invoice describing what I did during that time. Often, I will wait until I hear from the client and received payment for my work to that point to resume working on the manuscript. Always I ask for feedback and I usually speak to the client on the phone to discuss the progress at least once a month.

The process and the editor/author communication go much more smoothly when there are frequent conversations. This personal contact by email, telephone, and actual face-to-face meetings help to make the connection more than just a business relationship. It helps to put the client at ease and to establish a climate of trust and a sense of partnership. It helps one to better understand the child when one has met the parent. The manuscript is the author's creation or "baby" and he naturally feels protective of it. This is another reason that I advocate editing as lightly as possible, trying not to change anything that changes the meaning, tone, or sense of the work.

The best praise I can get is when an author says, "I don't see what you changed. It just seems to read more smoothly." I particularly like it when an author tells me after I have completed the editing of his entire manuscript, "I didn't realize that I was such a good writer." When he says that I simply smile and say, "Yes, you are."

# ❧9❧

## *The Well-Rounded Editor*

A dedicated freelance editor will likely find that his job goes beyond merely editing the manuscript. Authors will often ask for advice on more than just word usage, spelling, grammar, format, and so forth. If they know that you have experience in fields other than the one in which you are currently working, that expertise might come into play as you interact with the client.

### THE EDITOR AS CONSULTANT

After a few years of editing I started to understand that the needs of most writers go beyond editing their manuscripts. They would benefit from an initial consultation where they could explain what kind of book they were writing and what they wanted to do with it. I was able after awhile to advise them and even help them learn more about writing and editing so that they wouldn't have to spend so much money on an editor. One would think that would defeat my purpose of making a living as an editor. After all, if they knew how to edit, would they even need me? The answer, I knew, was yes, they certainly would. Every writer needs an editor who can look at their writing with an objective eye. And unless a writer is a professional editor, he won't be able to edit his book according to book publishing standards. One doesn't become an editor overnight.

I began doing more and more consultations and started conducting seminars and writing workshops. These were based on what I learned about a writer's needs. What follows are some of the subjects that I believe editors could help their clients with.

## EDITING, REVISING, AND REWRITING

Whenever I get a manuscript that is not ready for professional editing, I send the writer back to the drawing board to do a rewrite with some of the following suggestions.

Authors must give their first draft room to breathe. After they finish writing, they should put the manuscript away and not look at it for at least two weeks. They need to give themselves time to rest and recover from the effort, time to forget a little of what they wrote, and time to let their unconscious mind work on it. When they feel that they can read it with fresh eyes—and not before—that's when they should begin editing and rewriting.

The major concern when you edit is what to take out and what to leave in. I start by telling the author to take out anything that is not needed. Unnecessary words are like weeds that must be pulled out to allow the sunshine in and the optimal product to appear. Does it really need all of those adjectives and qualifiers? Take them out and reread the sentence. They may find that the sentence is more powerful without them.

### Show, don't tell

Some authors have asked me, "How do you do that?" I answer, "Well, think action and dialog when you are writing. Don't tell what the person is feeling, for example, but show what the character does. Instead of writing that he felt sad, describe his face with tears welling in his eyes, his chin quivering. Have her say how she feels: "I don't even want to get out of bed in the morning."

## Overwriting

This includes over-explaining anything, whether it's a character or incident in a novel or a lesson or principle in a nonfiction book.

- After the author has presented an idea, be sure he doesn't go on and on explaining what he means.
- Get rid of any text that does not advance the ideas or the story.
- Everything in the book should have a reason to be there. That includes the characters.
- Minor characters often enhance a story but they should also advance it. If they don't have some connection or interaction with the protagonist or other major characters, they have no business there.
- Scenes should not be overly long and drawn out. Don't let the characters overstay their welcome. Let them do their deed, speak their piece, and move on.
- Check to see if the dialog is the way we speak, in short sentences using common language. If a character's speech takes up more than ten lines or so, it may be too long.

As you change things, read them aloud to yourself. If you stumble over a word or hear unnatural dialog, you will know that you don't yet have it right.

## Repetition

Assume the reader is intelligent and will get the idea the first time it is presented. The writer may elaborate on a point, but should avoid repeating it using the same words. It is hard to remember exactly what you read in previous pages. If you are in doubt, click *Edit, find* in your Word program and type in some key words to see if it is a repeat.

## Redundancies

Watch for phrases such as *actual fact, revert back, sum total, protrude out, regular routine, baby kitten,* and *resume again.* Those word pairs are synonyms; only one is necessary.

## Consistency

- Check for tense. If the author is writing in past tense, be sure that he doesn't slip into present tense.
- Be sure the writer is consistent in his writing style. Whether he chooses a formal or a more conversational approach he must maintain that style throughout the book.
- Beware of a manuscript that calls a character Aunt Bertha in the first few pages and Aunt Betsy later on. Find out which name the writer wants to use and be sure it is consistent throughout the book.
- Check the spelling of words that can be spelled more than one way correctly, and that includes characters' names such as *Steven, Stephan,* and *Stephen;* and *Sherry* and *Cherie;* and *Betty, Bettye,* and *Bette.* And, again, be sure they are consistent throughout the book.

## Complex sentences and words

Advise the writer to avoid long sentences as well as a lot of short choppy sentences. Suggest he vary the length of them and not try to get too many ideas into one sentence. Break very complex sentences into two simpler sentences. Also limit jargon and a string of polysyllabic words.

## Spelling

Turn spell-check on because it will help you catch misspellings, but beware of words it won't help with, such as using *their* when it should be *there*. Watch for frequently confused words such as *bazaar* and *bizarre, apprize* and *appraise, retch* and *wretch*. Keep a dictionary handy and look up everything you aren't sure of.

## BRING YOUR EDITING UP TO DATE

Language has changed a lot in the past decade or so. Due to the blizzard of words that pass back and forth over the Internet every day, informal written communication has become more casual and spontaneous. There was a time when writing and speaking were two very different forms of communication but that has changed. The written word has become more conversational, and in nearly all fields of writing.

To reach the general reading audience, we need to write more like we would speak. A distinction must still be made between formal and informal writing. Scientific papers, doctoral dissertations, and articles for some periodicals still require strict adherence to formal standards, but even formal writing is changing in the interest of clarity and readability.

Many of the old rules have been relaxed and, like it or not, if we doggedly stick to the old ways of writing, we are going to seem stodgy. This is not to say we can now forget all the old rules of grammar and sentence structure. There are standards that must be maintained as they are necessary to good writing. But there are some rules that can be broken and here are a few of them.

The word *whom* has gone almost completely out of style and most dictionaries now state that in informal usage, *who* serves in most cases. *Whom* is still properly used after a preposition: *to whom, for whom, by whom,* for example, but although we would say *to whom did you give it?* it's okay to say *who did you give it to?* This usage also breaks the old rule of never ending a sentence with a preposition but we never worry about that anymore.

Is it *none is* or *none are*? Since the ninth century *none* has been used with both singular and plural verbs. Thus, either verb is acceptable.

And what about *different from* versus *different than* and *compare to* versus *compare with*? Both forms are now considered standard usage.

Even the spelling of plurals has changed. In many current books you will now see *appendixes* instead of *appendices, memorandums* rather than *memoranda, millenniums* not *millennia,* and *symposiums* in place of *symposia.*

Which is correct, *an historical building* or *a historical building*? The new rule is that you use "an" if the start of the next word has a vowel sound. *Historical* is not pronounced *istorical*. We hear the *h,* a consonant sound, so it is *a historical,* not *an historical.*

## LIMIT THE USE OF ADJECTIVES, ADVERBS, AND QUALIFIERS

As an editor you will need to watch for the writer's overuse of unnecessary words. Through taking out most adjectives, adverbs, and qualifiers, you can make the writing stronger. Some, of course, are necessary, but using too many of them brands the writer as a novice. An adjective modifies a noun by limiting, qualifying, or specifying. It is distinguished by having comparative and superlative endings like *–able, –ous, –er, –est.* Qualifiers are words like *rather, quite, very,* and *little.* An adverb is distinguished by the ending *–ly.*

To quote from *The Elements of Style,* "Write with nouns and verbs, not with adjectives and adverbs. The adjective hasn't been built that can pull a weak or inaccurate noun out of a tight place . . . it is nouns and verbs, not their assistants, that give good writing its toughness and color." Stephen King believes that "the road to hell is paved with adverbs."

Overwriting is fine for the first draft but deadly in the final draft. Encourage your client to write concisely. If you find him often writing "in other words," he is probably writing too much. To again quote *The Elements of Style,* "A sentence should contain no unnecessary words for the same reason that a machine should have no unnecessary parts."

Simplifying our language and adapting our words to the modern reader's vocabulary is not "writing down" to the reader, it is making our writing clearer and more interesting.

Thousands of new words are added to our dictionaries every year. Many nonstandard words have become standard as a result of frequent usage. To reach today's audience, we must bring our writing into the 21st century. So help the writer toss out antiquated expressions, out-dated ideas, and old rules, and keep his writing fresh. No one wants to read material that appears dated.


## STAY WITHIN YOUR COMFORT ZONE

Before you take on a new project—or continue editing the one you are on now—be sure that you are qualified to edit the kind of manuscript that has been presented to you. Recently, a client asked me to edit, design the pages, and typeset a children's picture book. At first I told myself I could do it although I had never worked on this kind of book before. Within a few hours I realized the client needed the services of an editor who had experience in that genre, and a designer who had the equipment and expertise to do a quality job of typesetting the many color drawings. I simply did not feel qualified to do it.

Taking on a job that was beyond my area of expertise was a mistake that I vowed never to make in the future. It was a disservice to both of us. I could not, in good conscience, continue and I certainly couldn't charge him for the time I had spent on it. I contacted my client and asked for a meeting. Telling him that he needed to find someone who could do justice to his book, I handed his work back to him and apolo-gized for accepting it in the first place. I expected him to be angry with me but he was very grateful that I was so honest with him. He has since recommended me to other writers who were writing the kinds of books I specialize in.

To avoid that kind of embarrassment ask yourself the following questions. If you cannot answer *yes* to all of them, think twice about accepting the job.

Am I familiar with the genre?

Do I have the experience, knowledge, and training to edit this kind of book?

Can I do a professional job of designing the pages?

Do I have the appropriate equipment and know how to use it?

## PREPARING A FINAL MANUSCRIPT FOR PRODUCTION

As an editor you may be asked to prepare the final manuscript for production. If you are not doing the page design, and most editors are not designers, you will have to follow the designer's layout or list of specifications. A manuscript consists of two levels of information: content and structure. The content includes the text and any figures that will appear in the published book, article, or report. The structure is the manuscript's component parts, such as heads and subheads, text, footnotes, illustrations, and tables.

If no list of specifications is available, you may need to mark up the hard copy indicating the basic layout. That will include showing where Roman page numbers and Arabic numbers begin. You will also have to explain whether or not the numbers will actually appear on the page. For example, no page numbers are on the title page, copyright page, and table of contents. If there is a half-title and the first chapter begins on page 3, "Arabic p. 3" should be noted at the chapter opening. You need to specify whether certain elements are to begin on a recto (right-hand page) or a verso (left-hand page). Usually, the page showing the part number (Part 1, Part 2, Part 3, etc.) goes on the recto as well as the first page of the chapter. You will need to check that all elements—that is, the front matter, the text, and the back matter—are in the correct order and that the order is reflected in the table of contents.

The editor may need to provide a list of copy for running heads (or feet). Running heads are the headings at the tops of pages that function as signposts. However, they may be omitted in a novel or a book of poems. If they are placed at the bottom of the page, they are called running feet. Running heads (or feet) are never used on display pages such as the title, copyright, dedication, or epigraph, or on the first page of the table of contents, preface, introduction, and so forth. The list should indicate which heads appear on the recto and which on the verso.

## PRODUCTION CHECKLIST

When the manuscript is ready to be typeset the editor needs to make a checklist of vital statistics that include information about how it is to be produced. The list might include the following information:

- Name of the author and title of the work
- A list of the parts of the project such as printout, illustrations, electronic files
- A list of codes, special fonts and characters, and special instructions
- A list of any material to come later
- An indication of how footnotes or endnotes are to be set
- A list of elements in the front matter, the text, and the back matter
- An indication of which elements must start recto
- An indication of how many paper sets of proofs should be produced

The typesetter may send you a cleaned-up version of the author's electronic files, converted, formatted and ready to edit, usually in a specific word-processing program. However, if you are familiar with the software you may be able to clean up and format the author's electronic files yourself. The following is a list of things you may need to do.

- Delete or fix extraneous spaces and tabs
- Change multiple hard returns to single hard returns

- Change underlining to italics. Examples of words that should be in italics are book titles, movie titles, television series titles, radio programs, plays, and newspapers. Some underlining may be appropriate, such as a collection that transcribes handwritten letters. If in doubt, check the *Chicago Manual* and discuss it with the author.
- Fix quotation marks and apostrophes.
- Fix commas and periods used in quotations. In most cases commas and periods go inside the quotation marks.
- See that em dashes and ellipses are used appropriately and consistently.
- Replace hyphens between numerals with en dashes.
- Convert footnotes to endnotes or endnotes to footnotes as is needed.
- Fix any els that are used as ones and any ohs that are used as zeros, and vice versa. The letter "l" and the number "1" may look alike in some fonts. The same is true for the letter "o" (lower case) and "O" (upper case) and the number "0" but they should not be used interchangeably.
- Adjust the line spacing, font, and margins and be sure that they are consistent throughout the manuscript.

Once this is done, print out a copy of the edited manuscript and mail it, or send it as an attachment to an email, to the author to review. Most authors want to see the final version and will be able to mark changes they wish to make on the printed copy with a red pen or pencil so that you can readily see them. After all the changes have been made and the book has been typeset and ready to be sent to the printer, an index—if the book is to have one—can be prepared and added to the final manuscript. As an editor, you may find it advantageous to learn how to organize and set up an index. This is another valuable service you can offer an author. At this stage you will have the correct page numbers for the book and can add them to the index.

A final proofreading should be done after the manuscript has been converted to its final form and the pages as well as the cover have been printed. This galley proof is checked against the final proofread copy before it was sent to the printer to be sure that the page numbers are correct in the index and that everything else checks out. The author should look at this, too, to be sure that everything is the way he or she wants it. At this point, the author is the one who bears the final responsibility for any errors in the published work.

# ❧ 10 ❧

## *The Business of Freelancing*

There is much more to making a living as a freelance editor than just being excellent at what you do. You must find the clients. You must establish your credentials. And you need to set up your business. You may have to rent office space. If you will be working out of your home you will have to know the regulations regarding a home office. In either case, cities often require you to have a business license. As each state has different rules and regulations, you will need to check with the city, county, and state in which you will be doing business.

### FICTITIOUS BUSINESS NAME

If you wish to use a fictitious business name you must file the name with a governmental agency, usually your county's recorder. This is also called a DBA (doing business as). You will have to check the records to be sure that the name you chose is not being used by someone else. Then you are required to publish the fictitious business name (FBN) in your local newspaper for a designated period of time. There is a charge for recording the FBN and another charge for publishing it in the newspaper.

## SELLER'S PERMIT

If you are selling items, your books for instance, you will have to have a seller's permit. You will have to do some research to find out how you get a seller's permit in your area. In some areas it is filed with the county; in others you might deal with the state government. In California you file with the California State Board of Equalization, Sales and Use Tax Department. Each year you must report your sales and pay any taxes that may be due. There is no charge for a seller's permit. To open a business account at your bank, you may be required to furnish both your approved fictitious business name and your seller's permit.

## ACCOUNTING

You may need legal advice as to what kind of business you are setting up. And if you don't already have a CPA who helps you with your taxes you may want to find one who will be able to give you financial advice and help you set up your accounting system for your business.

Self-employment offers you many opportunities for tax write-offs. You may be able to deduct your car (or your gasoline), telephone, Internet service, restaurant meals, office supplies and equipment, postage, magazines and journals, reference books, and even travel if it is business-related. You can deduct the costs for the classes and seminars you take. If you have a home office you can deduct a portion of your rent or mortgage payment and your utilities.

## SMALL BUSINESS RESOURCES

## SCORE

For business advice there is a terrific organization called SCORE. They call themselves "Counselors to America's Small Business." With offices nationwide, they are the premier source of free and confidential advice for entrepreneurs. They offer guidance online and in-person at one of their 364 offices nationwide. You can choose a mentor online and ask him or her your questions. You can make an appointment with a local mentor or attend a workshop. You can even take an online workshop or register for a lunchtime webinar. A nonprofit organization, SCORE is dedicated to educating entrepreneurs and helping small businesses start, grow, and succeed nationwide. Over 13,000 volunteers consisting of both working and retired executives and business owners donate their time and expertise as business mentors. SCORE is a resource partner with the U.S. Small Business Administration (SBA). You might want to sign up for their eNewsletter for tips, trends, and success secrets. For more information you can contact the SCORE organization at 1-800-634-0245 or go to their website at www.score.org.

## Small Business Administration (SBA)

Another resource is the U.S. Small Business Administration. It has delivered millions of loans, loan guarantees, contracts, counseling sessions, and other forms of assistance to small businesses. Among the services it provides are business financing from the smallest needs in micro-lending to investment (venture) capital. It also provides free individual face-to-face and Internet counseling and low-cost training to entrepreneurs and established small businesses. For more information on the Small Business Administration write to the SBA at 409 3rd Street, SW, Washington DC 20416 or call the SBA Answer Desk at 800/827-5722. Website: www.sba.gov. Email them at answerdesk@sba.gov.

## Small Business Development Center (SBDC)

Small Business Development Centers (SBDCs) are partnerships primarily between the government and colleges/universities administered by the Small Business Administration, and they aim at giving educational services for small business owners and aspiring entrepreneurs.

They are located in all fifty states as well as the District of Columbia, Puerto Rico, and the U.S. Territories, and are operated statewide or at a state region-wide level. The lead organization coordinates program services offered to small businesses through a network of subcenters and satellite locations in each state.

Each center has a director, staff members, volunteers and part-time personnel. SBDC services include, but are not limited to, assisting small businesses with financial, marketing, production, organization, engineering and technical problems and feasibility studies. All services given at SBDCs are free and confidential, and additional low-cost training options are available.

Assistance from an SBDC is available to anyone interested in beginning a small business for the first time or improving or expanding an existing small business, who cannot afford the services of a private consultant.

For more information and to find a center in your area, go to www. sba.gov/content/small-business-development-centers-sbdcs.

## LEGAL GUIDES

The following books will help you with your legal questions. Although there may be times you will have to consult with an attorney, these books will give you a lot of information you should know before you go into business for yourself.

For general legal information, the books by Nolo Publishing are excellent. Their website is www.nolo.com. The Nolo company was formed to help people who couldn't afford the costs of a lawyer find information in many different fields of law. They call it do-it-yourself law. Among the books that may be of interest to you are *The Legal Guide for Starting and Running a Small Business* and *Working for Yourself,* which is listed as an all-in-one guide for the self-employed. You can purchase these books from the Nolo website.

Their books contain a great deal of excellent information including how to obtain licenses and permits, comply with IRS rules, and record-keeping, as well as legal forms you can copy and use for your purposes. I can recommend their books because I have used them myself. Most recently, I bought *How to Form a Nonprofit Corporation in California* and followed its directions when Tom Berg and I formed the California Literary Arts Society. I won't say it was easy but the information was clear and up to date and we were able to fill out all the forms necessary to get our 501(c)(3) nonprofit status. When we had questions we couldn't find answers to, we contacted the Internal Revenue Service personally and asked them for help. Believe it or not, there are real people who work for the IRS and they are happy to assist you. Governmental entities are often the best source for accurate legal information because, after all, they made the rules.

## Other resources

There is a great deal of information on the Internet that gives job descriptions, explains what is expected of an editor in various fields, and tells you how to price your work and get more training, and many of them even have job listings. There are organizations you can join and instruction manuals you can buy.

As you research websites, you will have to figure out what information is valid and what is some kind of sales pitch. Look for the sites that have name recognition. Don't rely on blogs, and don't use Wikipedia as an authority, because it isn't. Searching for authentic and useful information on the Internet is like looking for a four-leaf clover in a field of weeds. First you must find a patch of clover. After that, it's just a matter of knowing how to count the leaves.

*The Writer's Market* published by Writer's Digest Books is one of the many books you should have in your bookcase if you will be writing or editing books, scripts, or articles for magazines and trade journals. It is issued annually. Always get the most up-to-date edition. You can also get instant access to thousands of editors and agents by logging onto their website, WritersMarket.com. As you are working with writers, it would be an important added service if you were able to help them get information on where and how to market what they write. Remember, your job is to help writers put out the best piece of work possible and, in many cases, help them find ways to sell their works. Their success is your success.

# ❧ 11 ❧

## *Preparing Your Office*

As is true in any business there are preparations you must make before you open your doors to new business and start working with clients. Much of the work you do as an editor can be done through the mail, Internet, and telephone. But there will be times when your clients will be coming to your office for consultations and to work with you on their manuscripts. It is important to create a pleasant professional atmosphere whether your office is in an office building or in your home.

My office is in my home and I really like it that way. The downside of working at home is that I have to keep it clean and tidy. Maybe that is really the upside because I doubt that I would keep my house as neat as I do if I didn't have to. And I do like to have nice surroundings. When I have a lot of clients and can easily afford it I hire a housekeeper to come in once a week to help me keep up with the housework.

### OFFICE FURNITURE AND EQUIPMENT

You will need to set up your office and acquire the tools you will use, such as computers and specialized computer programs. As I have always worked out of my home, whenever I moved I made sure that I would have a separate room for an office that was large enough to accommodate all of the furnishings I needed. Generally what is required is some or all of the following:

- computer
- high-volume laser printer
- all-in-one inkjet color printer that can scan, copy, print, and fax
- large desk with two small drawers and a legal-sized file drawer
- computer desk
- filing cabinet
- comfortable, adjustable office chair
- guest chair for a client
- supply cabinet and/or shelves (if your office is in a bedroom, supplies can be in a closet)
- bookcase
- utility table that can accommodate items you don't want on your desk
- telephone (you might want both a land line and cell phone)
- paper cutter
- three-hole punch
- stapler
- lamps, a trash can, rolodex, etc.
- postage scale

## "Desktop Post Office"

As time is money to the freelance editor, here is a way to save a lot of it. The U.S. Postal Service now offers what they call a "Desktop Post Office." You can now avoid a trip to the post office by signing up with Stamps.com whereby you can use your computer to buy and print postage in any amount or mail class and you will get free delivery confirmation service with Priority Mail. You can weigh your mail on the digital scale they provide and print the postage on envelopes, labels, or plain paper. Stamps.com furnishes some labels at the beginning; afterward you will have to buy them but they aren't very expensive and it is a convenience. You can then drop your mail into a mail collection box or hand it to your postal carrier.

You can try it at no risk. You will also receive discounts you can't get at the Post Office. If you have been leasing a postage meter you won't have that expense anymore. In early 2011 I took advantage of their offer which was an $80 value, with $25 in postage, a $5 supplies kit, and a $50 digital postage scale. After a few months I had a problem with the scale, which stopped working, but I called Stamps.com and they sent me a new one (also at no cost) which has worked fine. For more information go to www.Stamps.com.

## CONSULTATIONS WITH CLIENTS

My dining area at the far end of my living room doubles as a conference room with a table and comfortable chairs. This is where I do consultations and work with writers on their manuscripts. It is more convenient than having my clients sit in a chair in my office because the table provides a hard surface we can use for making notes and working with manuscript pages. It is also a more attractive area with large sliding glass doors that look out on my back yard.

Since I don't have children living at home, my place is quiet and I can work undisturbed with my clients. If the meeting is going to take longer than a few minutes, I can offer them tea or coffee and I usually have some cookies or hard candy around to give both of us a bit of a sugar boost.

You may wish to have two phone numbers, one for personal use and one for business, but, depending on your type of clientele, you may need only one. Your phone will have to have call waiting and either an answering machine on your desk or an answering service provided by your telephone company. If you do not choose to give everyone your home address you may want to have a post office box dedicated to your business.

## OFFICE SUPPLIES

It's best to stock up before you begin your new career as a freelance editor. There are things you know that you will need. Among them are the following:

- letter size paper, 8½ x 11 inches, some of it 20 pound copy paper, some a higher grade of 24 pound paper. Buy it by the case; it's cheaper that way and you won't risk running out of it in the middle of a project.
- note paper and small notepads with an adhesive strip on the back
- paper clips, fasteners (for three-hole-punched paper)
- #2 pencils and pens in two colors. Mechanical pencils are best and you need both black ink pens which are best for legal documents and red ink pens for your editing notes.
- hanging file folders for the file cabinet and manila folders
- #9 and #10 business envelopes. The smaller envelope will fit inside the larger one; put your name and address on the front of the #9 and insert it with your invoice for your client to send your check. If you want to make it even more convenient for your client to pay your invoice right away, put a stamp on the return envelope.
- large manila envelopes

# ◆12◆

## *What Should You Charge?*

Whether you are launching your career as a freelance writer or editor, or a combination of both, figuring out what to charge is challenging. At first you don't want to charge so much that you will scare away clients so you may set your rates at the low end of the scale. I did it that way the first time I edited a book. That was about twenty years ago and I charged my first client $15 an hour. However, as other clients came along and I got busier, I kept raising my rate to a level where I could make a living at it. With more experience I edited faster; I didn't have to stop and look up as many things in *The Chicago Manual of Style*. So my expertise became even more valuable as time went on. Raising my rates did not seem to affect the number of clients I worked for. I just attracted a different kind of clientele: more serious writers and more professional people in higher income brackets.

There are a number of places where you can research the going rates for the services you provide. *The Writer's Market* has a section called "How Much Should I Charge" and, in addition to writing, it lists freelance editing services in various fields. This information is also on the Internet and I checked the lists of other resources. Some charge by the hour or minute, some by the word or page, and some by the project. Many editors have only an hourly rate. The following are some of the fees listed in various publications, organizations, and websites.

## Magazines and Trade Journals

Content Editing: $25 to $125 per hour, $2,000 to $6,500 per project, 6¢ to 15¢ per word

Proofreading: $15 to $55 per hour

## Newspapers

Copyediting: $15 to $35 per hour

Editing/Manuscript Evaluation: $25 to $75 per hour

## Medical/Science

Editing: $21 to $125 per hour, $3 to $12.50 per page, $500 to $600 per day

Proofreading: $18 to $125 per hour, $2.50 to $3 per page

## Book Publishing

Anthology Editing: $23 to $80 per hour; $1,200 to $7,900 per project

Content Editing (scholarly/textbook): $20 to $125 per hour, $500 to $15,000 per project, $3 to $20 per page, 5¢ to 10¢ per word

Content Editing (trade): $20 to $125 per hour, $1,000 to $20,000 per project, $3.75 to $20 per page, 5¢ to 10¢ per word

Copyediting (trade): $16 to $100 an hour, $2,000 to $5,500 per project, $1 to $6 per page, 3¢ to 6¢ per word

Personal History: $30 to $125 per hour, $750 to $40,000 per project

Proofreading: $15 to $40 per hour, $2 to $5 per page, 1¢ to 3¢ per word

Structural Editing: $25 to $120 per hour, $2,500 to $50,000 per project, 6¢ to 15¢ per word

Review and Critique: 40,000-word manuscript, $400 to $850; 80,000-word manuscript, $900 to $1,500. These are averages;

the charges may be less or more depending on the complexity of the manuscript, and the expertise of the reviewer.

## Other

Nonprofit Editing: $25 to $125 per hour
Advertising Editing: $20 to $125 per hour; 25¢ to $1 per word
Speech Writing/Editing: $35 to $167 per hour, $1,200 to $7,900 per project; $100 to $350 per minute
Business editing (general): $25 to $150 per hour
Corporate Periodicals: $35 to $125 per hour; 75¢ to $2.50 per word
Newsletters: $25 to $125 per hour, $150 to $230 per page
Government Agency Editing: $20 to $100 per hour, 25¢ to $1.25 per word
Government Grant Writing/Editing: $19 to $150 per hour
Technical Editing: $25 to $150 per hour
Web Editing: $25 to $100 per hour, $3 to $10 per page
Picture Editing: $40 to $100 per hour, $35 to $65 per picture

In researching medical and science editing websites I found an average editing fee of $70 per hour. Some charge more for rush or same-day services. Some charge an additional administrative fee per order. Bio-Science Writers estimates the number of pages that can be edited in an hour. For basic services it is 4 to 5 pages an hour; for advanced, 3 to 4 pages per hour; and for professional, 2 to 3 pages per hour.

The decision of what to charge for your services is not an easy one to make, especially when your are just starting out. If you charge a very low fee, prospective clients might think that you are not qualified enough to charge the going rate, and they could undervalue your expertise. If you charge a very high fee, it could turn away writers who cannot afford you. Try setting your fee somewhere in the middle of the range and see what happens. You can always adjust your rates upward or downward at a later date.

# ᔧ13ᖼ

## *Legal Matters*

There aren't as many legal concerns for freelance editors as there are for writers. Editors are not held responsible for any libel, slander, plagiarism, or copyright infringements that might appear in a document she is editing. The author is responsible for that. And as an editor, you cannot be expected to offer legal advice to your writer/client. In fact, it would be unethical to do so unless you are also an attorney.

However, writers need to know their rights and how to protect their works. They also need to be alerted to the possibility that they may be violating another's rights. If you, as an editor, have noticed text that raises a red flag, it is your duty to your client, I believe, to mention it to him. You may help him avoid an embarrassing accusation of defamation and a possibly costly lawsuit. According to attorney Tad Crawford, "Most authors have more to fear from defaming others than being defamed."

In *The Writer's Legal Guide: An Authors Guild Desk Reference* by Tad Crawford and Kay Murray (published by Allworth Press and The Authors Guild), defamation, libel, and slander are explained very clearly. Defamation is defined as "The publication of a false statement of fact about a person or organization, in writing, visually, or verbally, that is derogatory and that injures the subject's reputation. The statement must reach at least one person other than the subject because damage to a reputation is the essence of defamation. If the statement is spoken, the defamation is deemed slander. If the statement is expressed visually, through words or images (including motion pictures), it is libel. In many states injury to a reputation is easier to prove when the claim is one of libel rather than slander."

There are writer's groups that help their members with individual business and legal advice and advocacy from experienced publishing attorneys. The Authors Guild is among the best of them. (See the Authors Guild listing under Professional Organizations.)

There are several books that cover important subjects such as copyright protection, fair use, permissions, libel, invasion of privacy, and resolving legal disputes, to name a few. Editors—and certainly writers—should have at least one of these references in her library.

Any information that is important for a writer to know is also important for an editor to know. This is especially true if you plan to also act as consultant to your clients. You can't be expected to know everything, particularly about legal matters, but it will be vitally helpful to your clients if you have some idea of what to look out for. *Publishers Weekly* called *The Writer's Legal Guide* "An indispensable handbook for anyone who writes." The *Guide* answers virtually every question writers are likely to face concerning their rights. The book also gives practical advice on how to establish a successful and profitable writing career.

Another book every editor should have in her library is *Business and Legal Forms for Authors and Self-Publishers* by Tad Crawford, Allworth Press. The forms it contains will give you a great deal of information on and examples of agreements that both you as an editor and your client as a writer need to know about and understand. Among the forms that may apply to your work with a writer and/or publisher are the Nondisclosure Agreement, Privacy Release, Contract with an Independent Contractor, and Estimate Form.

## OTHER LEGAL REFERENCES

***The Writer's Legal Companion: The Complete Handbook for the Working Writer*** by Brad Bunnin. Perseus Books

***The Copyright Permission and Libel Handbook: A Step-by-Step Guide for Writers, Editors, and Publishers*** By Lloyd J. Jassin and Steven C. Schecter. Wiley Books

## COPYRIGHT INFRINGEMENT

Exploiting the exclusive rights of copyright without the owner's permission is considered copyright infringement. All lawsuits involving copyright are brought in federal court. The penalties can be severe, and include restraint from further use of the work, destruction of unauthorized copies, and money damages. The claimant must prove that he owns the copyright, and the certificate of registration provides presumptive proof.

## FAIR USE

The fair use doctrine is the most important limitation on the owner's exclusive rights. A fair use claim is hard to apply. It has been called "so flexible as virtually to defy definition." Four factors are weighed to determine whether a use is fair. They are:

- The purpose and character of the use, including whether the use is of a commercial nature or for nonprofit educational purposes
- The nature and character of the copyrighted work
- The amount and substantiality of the portion used in relation to the copyrighted work as a whole
- The effect of the unauthorized use on the market for or value of the copyrighted work

The purpose of the fair use doctrine is to avoid an application of the copyright laws that might restrict the growth of knowledge. An infringement is not based on the number of words copied or quoted from other works, as some people believe. There are so many factors considered as to make any clear definition of fair use difficult. To ascertain whether that which is being copied is truly "fair use" it would be best to seek the advice of an attorney.

## PERMISSION

Even if an author has a contract with a publisher, clearances are generally the responsibility of the author, and that often includes payment for the license fees. Works published in the United States before January 1, 1923 are in the public domain. If they are published between January 1, 1923 and December 31, 1977 they are protected by copyright for ninety-nine years from the date of publication. If you aren't sure that a work is in the public domain you should find that out. To be on the safe side, always try to get permission.

First you must determine who is the owner of the material you wish to copy or quote. For books, the publisher's address will be on the copyright page. If you don't have access to the book itself, you can find the information in *The Literary Market Place* (LMP). It is published by R.R. Bowker and most public libraries will have it. If not, they will probably have *Books in Print* which is a master guide to publishers, authors, and book titles. Often, these references are on their computers and you can have direct access to the databases.

In some cases, you may be able to obtain copyright permission from a photocopying service which will add the price of license fees, if there are any, to the cost they are charging you for the copies.

Here are several other ways to search for the owner of the copyright:

- The Copyright Clearance Center (www.copyright.com). If they are able to give permission they will quote a charge.

- The Copyright Office (www.loc.gov/copyright/). All recorded assignments and licenses from January 1, 1978 to the present can be found and searched free of charge, twenty-four hours a day. However, if a copyright has not been registered with the Copyright Office, that doesn't mean it is not protected by copyright, only that it is not in their records.
- The Authors Registry (www.authorsregistry.org). This is a clearing house for payments to authors. The Registry has a database with contact information for more than thirty thousand authors.
- For song lyrics, contact one of the following:
  ASCAP, the American Society of Composers, Authors and Publishers, (323) 883-1000, email: info@ascap.com; Website: www.ascap.com
  BMI, Broadcast Music, Inc. (212) 586-2000 (New York); or (310) 659-9109 (Los Angeles). Website: www.bmi.com.

These are the two major music performance rights associations. They can tell you how to find the publisher of the songs. However, they cannot grant permission to quote lyrics.

- For animated cartoon characters and other copyrighted works that are licensed through film studios or television production companies, check The Hollywood Creative Directory or call (323) 525-2369. Website: www.hcdonline.com. It lists the names of production companies, TV shows, and studio personnel.
- To locate a syndicated or editorial cartoonist, contact the Graphic Artists Guild (212) 791-3400. Website: www.graphi-cartistsguild.org.

To get permission, write a letter to the copyright owner explaining what your project is and what material you want to use, the extent of the rights you need, and the credit line and copyright notice you will give. You may have to pay a fee for the permission but fees are nego-

## SAMPLE PERMISSION FORM

[Your name] (the "Licensee") is researching, writing and publishing a book [or an article] tentatively entitled [Title] (the "Work") to be published by [Publisher]

For valuable consideration [describe fee or free copies of the book, although sometimes neither is necessary], [Owner's name] (the "Licensor") grants the Licensee the [non-]exclusive right to reproduce the following material (the "Material") in the Work in [specify medium or format, language(s), territory, time period, if any]:

Titles: _____

Author: _____

Publisher: _____

Pages and/or lines: _____

Licensee shall not alter the Material without the prior written permission of the Licensor, and the Licensee shall include proper copyright notice and the following credit line in all versions of the Work:

_____.

Licensor warrants that [s]he has the sole and unrestricted right to make the grant contained in this agreement.

_____        _____
Licensor                                 Date

_____        _____
Licensee                                 Date

tiable and often depend on the amount and nature of the material you wish to use.

## PRIVACY AND RELEASES

Your author/client may wish to include photographs of people in her work and you should advise her that there is a risk of violating their rights to privacy and publicity. Examples of violations to the right to privacy include the following:

- the use of a person's name, portrait, or picture for the purpose of advertising or trade
- the use of a celebrity's image for commercial gain
- public display of an image that shows or implies something embarrassing or untrue
- physically intruding into a private space such as a home or office to take a photograph

It is not an invasion of privacy to use people's images for newsworthy and editorial purposes. That is protected by the First Amendment. No releases are required for uses which serve the public interest.

If there is a possibility of commercial use of the photograph, a release should be obtained. Even though some states may not require a written release or a payment for the use of a photograph, the author would be wise to get permission in writing and, in some cases, offer to pay for the use of the photo. The release is intended to cover only one use. If the image is used again for a different purpose, the release may not protect the author.

A minor in a photograph must have a parent or guardian give consent. In most states, the age of majority is eighteen.

# Privacy Release Form

Authors and self-publishers often accompany writing with photographs of people. Both text and photographs (or other images of people) raise the risk of violating an individual's rights to privacy and publicity. While these laws are intricate, this summary will help alert the author to potential dangers.

The right to privacy can take a number of forms. For example, state laws and court decisions forbid the use of a person's name, portrait, or picture for purposes of advertising or trade. This raises the question of the definitions for the terms "advertising" and "trade." Public display of an image which showed or implied something embarrassing and untrue about someone would also constitute a violation of the right to privacy. And physically intruding into a private space such as a home or office, perhaps to take a photograph for use with an article, can be an invasion of privacy.

The right of publicity is the right which a celebrity creates in his or her name, image, and voice. To use the celebrity's image for commercial gain violates this right of publicity. And, while the right of privacy generally protects only living people, a number of states have enacted laws to protect the publicity rights of celebrities even after death. These state laws supplement court decisions which held that celebrities who exploited the commercial value of their names and images while alive had publicity rights after death.

On the other hand, use of people's images for newsworthy and editorial purposes is protected by the First Amendment. No releases need be obtained for such uses, which serve the public interest.

What should the author do about all this? If the author is certain that the image will only be used for newsworthy and editorial purposes, no privacy release need be obtained. This should cover most of the images used by authors. If, on the other hand, there is a possibility of commercial use, a release should be obtained. For example, a photograph can be used for posters, postcards, and T-shirts, all of which are clearly trade uses. Or the photograph can be used in an advertisement. Only by having a privacy release can the author ensure the right to exploit the commercial value of the image in the future.

Form 9 allows the author to use a person's image for advertising and trade. While some states may not require written releases or the payment of money for a release, it is always wise to use a written release and make at least a small payment as consideration. By the way, Form 9 is intended for use with friends and acquaintances who pose, as well as with professional models or people connected with a piece of writing.

It is also important to be aware that if the release is intended to cover one use, and the image is then used in a distorted and embarrassing way for a different purpose, the release may not protect the author, regardless of what it says. An example of this would be a privacy release signed by a model for a bookstore's advertisement, in which she was to appear in bed reading a book. This advertisement was later changed and used by a bedsheet manufacturer known for its salacious advertisements. The title on the book became pornographic and a leering old man was placed next to the bed looking at the model. This invaded the model's privacy despite her having signed a release.

In general, a minor must have a parent or guardian give consent. While the author should check the law in his or her state, the age of majority in most states is eighteen.

The author should have any release signed at the same time the image is obtained. If the author, for example, is taking photographs, the privacy release should be signed during the session. While a witness isn't a necessity, having one can help if a question is later raised about the validity of the release.

If the author is asked to use a release form supplied by someone else, the author must make certain that the form protects the author. The negotiation checklist will be helpful in reviewing the provided form and suggesting changes to strengthen the form.

Is a privacy release necessary when an author wants to have exclusivity with respect to a newsworthy story? It is not, because this exclusivity is obtained by entering into an agreement between the author and the person who is the subject of the story or knows the information to be contained in the story. This might take the form of a collaboration agreement, but it might also take the form of an agreement to provide information only to the author in return for some compensation. Since the information is newsworthy, no privacy release need be obtained. However, the exclusivity provision that appears in the other provisions with Form 6 would be appropriate to use (changing the word "coauthor" to suit the circumstances) and the provisions of the privacy release might be added as an extra safeguard.

## Filling in the Form

Fill in the dollar amount being paid as consideration for the release. Then fill in the name of the person giving the release and the name of the author. Have the person and a witness sign the form. Obtain the addresses for both the person and the witness and date the form. If the person is a minor, have the parent or guardian sign. Have the witness sign and give the addresses of the witness and the parent or guardian as well as the date.

## Negotiation Checklist

❑ Be certain that some amount of money, even a token amount, is actually paid as consideration for the release.

❑ Have the release given not only to the author, but also to the author's estate and anyone

else the author might want to assign rights to (such as a manufacturer of posters or T-shirts).

❑ If someone else has obtained the release, be certain that it covers successors and assigns such as the author.

❑ State that the grant is irrevocable.

❑ Cover the use of the name as well as the image of the person.

❑ Include the right to use the image in all forms, media, and manners of use.

❑ Include the right to make distorted or changed versions of the image as well as composite images.

❑ Allow advertising and trade uses.

❑ Allow any other lawful use.

❑ Have the person waive any right to review any finished artwork, including written copy to accompany the artwork.

❑ Have the person recite that he or she is of full age.

❑ If the person is a minor, have a parent or guardian sign the release.

## NONDISCLOSURE AGREEMENT

Some ideas have such promising commercial value that to share them with anyone presents a risk of their getting stolen. Since one can't copyright an idea, what can an author do to protect his idea for an image, format, product, story, television series, or other creation? He can use a nondisclosure agreement, which creates an express contract between the person disclosing the idea and the person receiving it.

As I mentioned in an earlier chapter, writers sometimes ask me to sign a nondisclosure agreement before I see the work I will be editing. They don't want me to discuss any facet of their book with anyone else. I am always happy to sign it. I also advise them to be cautious if anyone else they may be showing their work to refuses to sign such a document.

Stealing an idea, even a fully realized idea, isn't a rarity in television or film. Entire scripts are sometimes stolen too, especially if the thief thinks that he or she can get away with it. Sometimes the person who steals it is a producer or director who is presented a spec script or treatment (synopsis of the story) by a writer who wants to sell it to him. Very often, companies (and producers) will refuse to sign a nondisclosure agreement. They have their own agreement they want the writer to sign. Their agreement protects themselves, of course, not the writer. The agreement might say that the company will not be liable for using a similar idea. They may place a maximum value on the idea of only a few hundred dollars, or less. They know that if a person wants to break into the exclusive world of entertainment as a writer badly enough, he will sign just about anything.

This is not to discourage anyone from presenting a nondisclosure agreement to a company and asking them to sign it, nor to advise against ever signing producers' agreements that protect them. Not all producers or companies are dishonest. Many have very good reputations. However, writers must be aware of the pitfalls and protect themselves as much as possible without making it impossible for a production company to work with them. A scriptwriter who has an agent will have more protection because it will be the agent who will present the idea or work on his behalf. At any rate, do register your work with both the U.S. Copyright office and the Writers Guild. Then you have a fighting chance of getting the credit for it and being paid.

Once again, here is a sample of the Nondisclosure Agreement for Submitting Ideas.

---

## Nondisclosure Agreement for Submitting Ideas

**W**hat can be more frustrating than having a great idea and not being able to share it with anyone? If the idea has commercial value, sharing it is often the first step on the way to realizing the remunerative potential of the concept. The author wants to show the idea to a publisher, manufacturer, or producer. But how can the idea be protected?

Ideas are not protected by copyright, because copyright only protects the concrete expression of an idea. The idea to write a guide to the White House is not copyrightable, but the written guide certainly is protected by copyright. The idea to have a television series in which each program would have a narrator teach local history at a well-known landmark in his or her locale is not copyrightable, but each program would be protected by copyright. Of course, copyright is not the only form of legal protection. An idea might be patentable or lead to the creation of a trademark, but such cases are less likely and certainly require expert legal assistance. How does an author disclose an idea for an image, a format, a product, or other creations without risking that the listener, or potential business associate, will simply steal the idea?

This can be done by the creation of an express contract, an implied contract (revealed by the course of dealing between the parties), or a fiduciary relationship (in which one party owes a duty of trust to the other party). Form 11, the Nondisclosure Agreement, creates an express contract between the party disclosing the idea and the party receiving it. Form 11 is adapted from a letter agreement in *Licensing Art & Design* by Caryn Leland (Allworth Press).

What should be done if a company refuses to sign a nondisclosure agreement or, even worse, has its own agreement for the author to sign? Such an agreement might say that the company will not be liable for using a similar idea and will probably place a maximum value on the idea (such as a few hundred dollars). At this point, the author has to evaluate the risk. Does the company have a good reputation or is it notorious for appropriating ideas? Are there other companies that could be approached with the idea, ones that would be willing to sign a nondisclosure agreement? If not, taking the risk may make more sense than never exploiting the idea at all. A number of steps, set out in the negotiation checklist, should then be taken to try and gain some protection. The author will have to make these evaluations on a case-by-case basis.

### Filling in the Form

In the Preamble fill in the date and the names and addresses of the parties. In Paragraph 1 describe the information to be disclosed without giving away what it is. Have both parties sign the agreement.

### Negotiation Checklist

❑ Disclose what the information concerns without giving away what is new or innovative. For example, "an idea for a new format for a series to teach history" might interest a producer but would not give away the particulars of the idea (i.e., using different narrators teaching at landmarks in different locales). (Paragraph 1)

❑ State that the recipient is reviewing the information to decide whether to embark on commercial exploitation. (Paragraph 2)

❑ Require the recipient to agree not to use or transfer the information. (Paragraph 3)

❏ State that the recipient receives no rights in the information. (Paragraph 3)

❏ Require the recipient to keep the information confidential. (Paragraph 4)

❏ State that the recipient acknowledges that disclosure of the information would cause irreparable harm to the author. (Paragraph 4)

❏ Require good faith negotiations if the recipient wishes to use the information after disclosure. (Paragraph 5)

❏ Allow no use of the information unless agreement is reached after such good faith negotiations. (Paragraph 5)

If the author wishes to disclose the information despite the other party's refusal to sign the author's nondisclosure form, the author should take a number of steps:

❏ First, before submission, the idea should be sent to a neutral third party (such as a notary public or professional authors' society) to be held in confidence.

❏ Anything submitted should be marked with copyright and trademark notices, when appropriate. For example, the idea may not be copyrightable, but the written explanation of the idea certainly is. The copyright notice could be for that explanation, but might make the recipient more hesitant to steal the idea.

❏ If an appointment is made, confirm it by letter in advance and sign any log for visitors.

❏ After any meeting, send a letter that covers what happened at the meeting (including any disclosure of confidential information and any assurances that information will be kept confidential) and, if at all possible, have any proposal or followup from the recipient be in writing.

Some producers simply refuse to read a script by an unknown writer. The writer has to have an agent present it and it is as hard to get an agent for TV and film writers as for book authors. I hope more writers will have the courage to protect their work and stand up for their rights. They certainly deserve to get credit for their creations.

For more information on all of the above documents as well as actual tear-out forms you can make copies of and use, get *Business and Legal Forms for Authors and Self-Publishers* by Tad Crawford.

# ↬14↫

## *Maintaining the Momentum*

When people ask me how I've made a living as a freelancer all these years, I tell them I really don't know. It amazes me that I have. I do work at it, though. I constantly look for new ways to attract clients and new ways to serve my clients. Although I started out doing just editing, I have become a book shepherd and a literary consultant. I have also added desktop publishing to my menu of services. Several times a year I conduct seminars and teach workshops in various venues and they are usually well attended. I provide detailed handouts so that the attendees don't have to take a lot of notes and they have expressed their appreciation.

I have taught workshops in college extension courses, at various book festivals, in public libraries, and other places where writers gather. Some of them are sponsored by nonprofit organizations and I donate a percentage of the proceeds to the organization. It is a win-win situation because I can promote my services and attract donations for the nonprofits. I not only benefit financially from the seminars but the nonprofit does too. The event provides a service to writers and lets them know what I do. Some of my clients have come from those workshops.

Perhaps your goal is to become an excellent editor and not to get involved in the publishing process except to help authors prepare their manuscripts so that they are worthy of being published. That is certainly a creditable goal and for the first few years of working as a freelance editor, that was the extent of my services.

One can be a freelance writer as well as a freelance editor. The two go together very well. When the editing work is slow, you can write and sell articles and other works. I think most if not all editors are also writers. I've written poetry and song lyrics, scripts, and magazine articles but didn't always get paid for them. And, although I edited for book authors, it never occurred to me that I would ever write a book myself. I considered the idea far out of my comfort (and talent) zone. However, it wasn't long after I started my freelance editing career that I wrote my first book and it got published. And this is how it happened. As I mentioned in my chapter on Getting Started, I had edited for a gynecologist and his nutritionist wife who were writing a book on premenstrual tension and menopause. They had been trying to get a literary agent interested in it but the agent said that they needed to get a qualified book editor to bring their manuscript up to professional book publishing standards before he would represent them.

The doctor hired me and after I finished editing the manuscript, the agent sent it out to several publishers, eventually getting them a book deal with Parker Publishing, an imprint of Simon & Schuster. Working on their book got me thinking about an idea I had on helping people stop smoking. In the past I had worked as a stop-smoking therapist for Schick Stop Smoking Centers and for the American Lung Association. A previous smoker myself, I had quit in my 30s on doctor's orders but it had taken me two years to finally become liberated from my addiction.

I asked my clients' agent if he would look at my book proposal for a stop-smoking book and the first three chapters I had written to see if I had a viable idea. After a quick glance at it, he told me that there were so many books on how to quit smoking that he didn't think my book would have a chance. He said, "Now if you can come up with a novel approach, something that is truly different and has some solid science behind it, maybe we could get a publisher interested."

So it was back to the drawing board. I went to a local hospital and asked if I could do some research in their medical library and they granted me permission. It was there that I discovered that women have a tougher time quitting than men do. And it's far more damaging to a woman's body to a man's. It is also responsible for an increase in miscarriages, stillborns, and sudden infant death syndrome. Wow! I'd never heard about that before. Getting women to quit smoking was more important than I had realized. And there were no books on the market addressing women's addiction to tobacco. Aha! I changed my focus. My book was going to be about how women could quit.

When the agent saw my new book proposal and the first three chapters I had written, he decided to represent me and sent the proposal out to five publishers. There were offers from two publishers and I chose the one with the largest advance against royalties. The owner of the publishing company, by the way, was a medical doctor. He knew the research I had done was based on creditable scientific studies. The publisher titled the book *A Woman's Way: The Stop-Smoking Book for Women* (WRS Publishing). After that, I wrote a booklet called *The Stop-Smoking Diet for Women,* which was published by Health Edco, a company that sells health education products. The little 28-page booklet sold far better than the book, mostly to hospitals, clinics, and doctor's offices.

A few years later I decided to self-publish the first edition of *Author's Toolkit* because I didn't believe I would find a publisher for it. Like books about smoking, there were many books written about writing books and the world didn't need one more, I figured. I wrote the book for my editing clients and workshop attendees because I believed it would help them write better and understand a bit more about the book publishing industry. I got 1,000 books printed, figuring they would last me for about five years or more. But I was very pleasantly surprised. The book got good reviews in *Library Journal* and *The Los Angeles Times* and I sold nearly 4,000 copies over the next 18 months. I learned from the wholesaler that most of them sold to libraries who wanted it for their collections. Not wanting to be in the business of selling books out of my home, I looked for an established publisher for the second edition and Allworth Press took it on. Allworth published the revised (second edition) in 2003 and the third edition in November 2010. As they say in the entertainment business, the book had legs.

Having had the experience of both finding a publisher for my books and self-publishing them, I started adding services for my editing clients. I help them with their query letters and book proposals as well as all the steps of forming a publishing company and publishing their books themselves.

As an editor, your clients might ask you to write their book proposal. When I get that request from my clients, and I get it often from book authors, I give them this book proposal outline and ask them if they would consider writing it themselves and then giving it to me to edit. That makes more sense than having the editor do it initially because the author already has much of the information required for the proposal. The following is a book proposal outline that I developed through researching what publishers want to see when they are presented with a manuscript or book idea that the author wants them to publish. I use this as a handout in my book proposal workshops. Whether you write the proposal or the author does, you can use this as a guide.

## THE BOOK PROPOSAL

A book proposal is like a business plan or project design. Authors would be ahead of the game if they prepared at least a brief version of their proposal before they even began writing. It can serve as a guide and a checklist of what one needs to do to write a book that has a good chance of selling well. This is essential whether the author is publishing her book herself or seeking a literary agent or publisher for it.

For nonfiction, you can send publishers a book proposal with sample chapters before you have completed your book. For novels, publishers usually want to see the entire manuscript. For both nonfiction and fiction, check Book Publisher listings in the latest edition of *Writer's Market* for submission guidelines. For more specific and updated information, go to the publisher's website.

As you go through the steps of writing the proposal you will learn:

- **how to focus on your subject.** If you have a descriptive title and can sum up your book in one short sentence, you probably have a clear idea of what your book is about.
- **how to describe your book to others.** By writing a synopsis, you will be able to get to the essence of the information contained in your book and explain it clearly.
- **how to organize your material.** Preparing a chapter-by-chapter outline of your book will help keep you on track as your write. It may also eliminate any potential "writer's block."
- **whether you have a salable idea.** As you research the market potential, you will find out if what you plan to write is likely to find a wide audience.
- **how to sell yourself.** When you tell about your background and promotional skills, you may discover that you need to do additional research in areas where you lack training or experience.
- **what your competition is.** If you find another book that is a great deal like your own, you may want to change yours in some way or re-think whether you even want to write it.

The proposal should be double-spaced with the exception of the Synopsis. On each page, place the section number and subject in the upper right corner. Below that put the title of your book and under that the page number in that section.

## I. Title Page

Do your best to get a hook into the title; something that will grab attention. You can add a subtitle that tells more about the book. Choose a title that has not been used before, if possible.

Study the subject guide to *Books in Print* for current titles. Also check *Forthcoming Books* for books that publishers have in the works.

Libraries usually have these lists on computer. Amazon.com does not have a complete list of titles in print, but their site can give you a good idea of what is out there. Go to a bookstore and look at other books similar to yours in some way.

On the Title Page, put your title, subtitle, if any, and your name as the author. Below that write a brief description of your book. List the number of words or pages you have written or expect to write.

## II. Synopsis

This is an overview or brief summary of the book and should be single-spaced. Open with a powerful statement, startling statistics, or shocking facts. Having a focused idea and being able to explain it in a few short paragraphs is essential. Tell the purpose of your book and what it will do for the reader. Make the synopsis not only informative but interesting.

The synopsis should have a beginning, middle, and end, just as your book does. Tell how your book opens, what it is about, and how it ends. You may want to give some of the highlights, specific events, dialogue, or unknown facts.

## III. Author Bio

This is a narrative statement of your qualifications, experience, and reasons for writing the book.

List other books and articles you have written and explain your promotional skills such as public speaking, television or radio appearances, or seminars you have conducted on the subject. Suggest the names of prominent figures or authorities who may endorse your book. If you already have contacted them and they have agreed, be sure to mention it.

If you are writing a book regarding a specific field of interest it will be important to show that you have training and/or experience in that field.

## IV. Market Potential

Research the demographics and statistics of potential readers. For example: "The number of women living with children whose father is absent is over 10 million." This number is significant if your book is about how a single mother can help her child feel secure.

If your book is about motorcycles, find out how many people own motorcycles and how many motorcycle clubs and dealers there are. Your book may sell through their clubs and stores.

## V. Competitive Works

Research other books on the same subject; this is your competition. Borrow or buy books which may be similar to yours and read them. Choose four or five and list each by title, author, publisher, the year published, the number of pages and the price. Write a brief synopsis of each one and explain how yours is different.

## VI. Chapter Outline

Prepare a Table of Contents with chapter titles (but no page numbers). Under each chapter title write a paragraph or two explaining what it is about. This indicates that you have a clear grasp of your subject and have planned exactly how and in what order you will present your information.

## VII. Additional Features

If you will have an appendix, index, glossary, illustrations, or graphics of any kind, mention them on the title page and list them in this section. Include examples.

## Sample Chapters

Send between one and three completed chapters, depending on what the publisher asks for. Always send the first chapter. Readers want to know what a book is about. You must grab their interest on the first page. Don't waste time on exposition, back story, or set up. Get right to the point. The other two chapters you submit should be the ones you believe are the most important or most interesting. If you have a great closing chapter, include it.

As you continue to pursue your career in freelance editing, you probably will be asked for help on other projects. Your career doesn't have to be focused on just one type of document or for individuals only.

There may be organizations you donate time to that could use your services not just as a volunteer but for other work they need done—and will pay you for it. Keep your eyes and ears open for opportunities to write and edit other kinds of documents. All companies and nonprofit organizations need to advertise, produce brochures, promote their goods and services, and produce in-house documents, forms, and other kinds of things. As an accomplished editor, you can edit these, too. Let them know what you do and explain that you write and edit as a profession. Be careful about donating your time to this kind of work. The more you donate, the more they will expect you to donate. It's okay to donate your time as a docent or host at one of their events but your professional editing and writing should be paid for. Interestingly, the organization will value it more if they are paying you. And they will see you as a professional, not as just a volunteer.

There are many ways you can provide your services to organizations. You can help them write and edit their marketing material. This could consist of membership drives, fundraising campaigns, and promotional materials for their events.

Businesses also can use your expertise in producing many different kinds of written materials. These could include direct sales appeals, newsletters and releases, advertising, public relations, and promotional programs. As these materials can come from many different departments in the company, you could work with department heads in editing their writing. Although an employee may be very good at their specialty, few people are also excellent writers. As an editor you can make their documents look like they were written by an expert.

There are millions of businesses of all sizes in the United States and all of them produce written materials. To get your foot in the door you must first identify potential clients. Learn all you can about companies in your area and start mailing out brochures, sales letters, and other written material to see who responds. Attend association meetings and conventions and talk to people, tell them what you do, exchange business cards, hand out your brochures, and collect names and phone numbers.

Keep in touch with your former employers. Since they know what you can do and you know the people there, they may want to use your services for special in-house projects. Also call your individual clients from time to time just to chat. They will be pleased that you were thinking of them. Find out what they are doing now and if they have any writing projects coming up. Most of my clients are individuals who are writing books. Surprisingly, I found that many of them are planning to write another book and would like to have a consultation with me about it. Many of my former clients know of others who are writing a book and need an editor. Calling people you have worked for reminds them of you, and they will likely want to recommend your services to their friends as a result.

Referrals are golden. Those clients who come to me because I was recommended by a friend of theirs turn out to be the best people to work with. They already know about my editing, my charges, and my other services such as helping them publish their book themselves. They have probably seen the book their friend published and are impressed by the professional quality of the publication.

## RESEARCHING

Another way you can be of service to writers is to do research. That can be tremendously helpful to a busy writer or to one who has an impending deadline with a lot of writing left to do. There are many different subjects that require researching. For example, if an author is writing a historical novel, he may need to know about the period in which the story takes place, the location, clothing styles, local customs, the political climate at the time, and on and on. In a historical novel the story is fiction but the setting must be based on actual places and include what was going on during the time setting of the novel. Some of the facts that may be pertinent to the story could be who was president at the time, what was the means of transportation, what was the climate like in that part of the country and at that time of year.

As an editor who has already been working with an author's manuscript, you will know the story and the things that are important to it historically. So you would be a natural choice to find pertinent information.

Frequently, when I edit a manuscript, I see information that I believe is faulty and I will check it out. It might be the spelling of the name of a city, or the birthplace of a famous person, or the actual date of an important event. If it is more complex than that I will tell the author of my concern and ask if she would like me to research it. Authors are always glad to know when they have been in error so that they can fix it.

Not only does researching add another dimension to your services, it increases the time you will have to spend working on the manuscript. Thus you will earn more than you would have otherwise.

# ⚜15⚜

## *Self-Publishing*

When you work with an author who does not have a deal with a publisher, inevitably you will be asked about self-publishing. Many authors are choosing to publish their works themselves, particularly in this economic climate where it is harder than ever to interest an established publisher in the works of an unproven writer.

The following information covers the steps authors need to take to publish their books themselves and your guidance in this matter will be invaluable to your client. This is where you can shine as a consultant.

### HOW TO PUBLISH YOUR BOOK YOURSELF

Although you must either do everything yourself or hire some professional help with some of it, you have complete control over your book. If your book sells well, you will get a larger percentage of sales by truly self-publishing than you will by using a self-publishing company or by having it published by an established book publisher. While self-publishing companies are easy to spot, a self-publisher may not be if the result is a professional-looking book.

As the publisher, you will have to have your book designed, both the cover and the interior, and have it typeset to send to the printer. It is essential that you have it edited even if you are a good editor yourself.

STARTING YOUR CAREER AS A FREELANCE EDITOR

It's too easy to miss your own mistakes. A qualified editorial consultant can help you through this process and you may be able to do much of the design and typesetting yourself.

You may not even need to produce a paper book. You can produce an e-book. They cost far less to produce than a regular book. One-third of the sales of John Grisham's recent novel, *The Confession,* were e-books. Sales of e-books were up 158 percent from the same period last year and there was a 40 percent decrease in hardcover sales. Last year e-book sales came to $966 million.

Many self-published books have done very well and paid back the costs of publishing many times over. Some of them have been sold to established publishers who breathed new life into them and brought their authors great acclaim. Even when a book doesn't sell a lot of copies it can bring tremendous satisfaction and a sense of accomplishment to an author.

A self-published book does not carry the stigma it once did. If one produces an interesting, high-quality, well-written book, it will command respect. And if it is professional looking, most readers will have no idea that it was published by the author himself.

## SETTING UP A PUBLISHING COMPANY

You may be able to form a publishing company without having to consult an attorney if you plan to be the sole owner. If it will be a partnership or you wish to form a corporation, you should seek legal advice. Once you have decided on a name for your company you must file the fictitious business name (FBN) with your county, checking their records to be sure that the name is not already in use. This is also called a DBA (Doing Business As). You will then have to publish the FBN in a local newspaper for a period of time. You may register more than one company if both addresses are the same. You must re-register and pay another fee if you move.

You'll need a sales tax permit (also called a Seller's Permit) to sell your books, which you can get from The Board of Equalization in your

190

area. Some cities require a business license. Check with your city's government offices regarding their requirements. If you have a tax accountant, you should check with him regarding any state and federal tax matters you might need to consider, such as paying taxes on the profits or taking a tax write-off for expenses.

## PREPARING A BOOK FOR PUBLICATION

For each book you publish you will need an ISBN (International Standard Book Number). You should also get your copyright registered with the U.S. Copyright Office. You will need an LCCN (Library of Congress Card Number). You should complete an "Advance Book Information" form so that your book will be listed in the databases *Books in Print* and *Forthcoming Books* that provide information to bookstores and libraries. You will also need a bar code if you plan to sell your books through retail establishments such as bookstores and gift shops.

These forms need to be completed and submitted in a specific order. For example, you'll need your ISBN before you apply for your LCCN. The following is a list of the forms with a brief explanation of each one.

### ISBN Publisher Prefix

The International Standard Book Number (ISBN) identifies books and book-like products published internationally. The United States ISBN Agency is the only source authorized to assign ISBNs to publishers located in the United States, U.S. Virgin Islands, Guam, and Puerto Rico. The ISBN establishes and identifies one title from one specific publisher and is unique to that edition. The purpose is to allow for more efficient marketing of products by booksellers, libraries, universities, wholesalers, and distributors.

Each ISBN now consists of thirteen digits. Once an ISBN number or group of numbers has been assigned to a publisher, the publisher can assign the number to its publications. ISBNs are usually sold in blocks of ten or more. If you will be publishing more than one book under your publishing company name, you should get a block of numbers. However, authors and self-publishers can now purchase a Single ISBN. A block of ten numbers is currently $245. It costs more if you want priority or express processing. The Single ISBN is $125.

ISBNs can be purchased online at www.MyIdentifiers.com, the new home of the U.S. ISBN Agency and Bowker Identifier Services. You can purchase a Single ISBN plus a bar code for $150. Please check these prices as they may have gone up since this book was published.

## Library of Congress Control Number

If you want to participate in the Preassigned Control Number Program, you must complete and submit an Application to Participate. When you are approved, an account number and password will be sent to you via email. Then you will log on to the PCN system and complete a Pre-assigned Control Number Application. The Library staff will assign a control number which you will print on the back of the title page (the copyright page) in the following manner: Library of Congress Control Number: 2010012345.

For more information go to pcn.loc.gov/pcn.

## Copyright

It is always a good idea to register your copyright. It is a form of intellectual property law that protects original works of authorship including literary, dramatic, musical, and artistic works, such as poetry, novels, movies, songs, computer software, and architecture. The original authorship appearing on a website may be protected by copyright. This includes writings, artwork, photographs, and other forms of authorship protected by copyright.

Copyright does not protect names, titles, slogans, or short phrases. However in some cases, these things, as well as an artistic logo may be protected as trademarks. Contact the U.S. Patent & Trademark Office,

800-786-9199, for more information. Their website is www.uspto.gov/ trademarks.

There are three ways to register your copyright, and three different fees.

(1) The least expensive way is to file online through the Copyright Office (eCO) online system. The filing fee is $35 for a basic claim and you can pay for it with a credit or debit card.

(2) If you can't or don't want to file electronically, you can register with Fill-In Form CO, which replaces Forms TX, VA, PA, SE, and SR. As it uses 2-D bar code scanning technology, the forms can be processed faster than paper forms filled in manually. Complete the form on your computer, print it out, and mail it with a check or money order and your deposit. The fee for a basic registration is $50.

(3) Paper versions of Form TX, which is for literary works, are still available but it is the most expensive way to file. The registration fee using paper forms is $65. These paper forms are not accessible on the Copyright Office website but you may write or call the Office and ask for them. Staff will send them to you by postal mail. Their telephone number is 202/707-3000. Fill out the form according to the instructions that come with them. Send the completed form, a copy of your manuscript, and a check for registration to

> Library of Congress
> Copyright Office
> 101 Independence Avenue, S.E.
> Washington, DC 20559-6000

The effective date of registration is the day the Copyright Office receives a complete submission in an acceptable form. You don't have to wait for your certificate to arrive before you publish your book. For more information and instructions on how to file your copyright by any of the above means, go to www.copyright.gov/register.

Scripts should be registered with the Writers Guild of America-West. This can be used as a supplement to registering your work with the Copyright Office. And, for maximum protection, I suggest you register your script in both places. WGAWRegistry.org is the official script and screenplay registration service and considered by many to be the world's number one intellectual property service.

Since 1927, the Writers Guild of America–West Registry has been the industry standard in the creation of legal evidence for the protection of writers and their work. When you register your script prior to submitting it to editors, agents, managers, or producers, you document your authorship on a given date should there be unauthorized usage. You do not need to be a WGAW member to use this vital Guild service. Registration is fast, easy, and convenient to register online. Each registration submission costs $20 (or $10 for WGA members in good standing).

The WGAW Registry is located at 7000 West Third Street, Los Angeles, CA 90048. You can register online at WGAWRegistry.org. The registration hours are 9:30 AM to 5:30 PM Monday through Friday. If you have questions you can call them at (323) 782-4500.

## Advance Book Information form

Go to www.bowker.com and complete the form online. They no longer print paper forms.

## Bar code

Most printing companies will furnish a bar code for your book for a small fee if you are having them print your book. This is probably the best and least expensive way to get a bar code.

## PROMOTING AND SELLING YOUR BOOKS

How you promote your book depends to a large extent on what your book is about. You may already know the target audience. For example, if it was about sports or sports figures, a sporting equipment and/or clothing stores might carry your books. Children's books could be sold in toy stores or children's clothing stores.

Getting reviews is an excellent way to promote without a great deal of work. Get a list of reviewers and send review copies of your book three to six months before it is released.

You can promote and sell your book on your own publishing company's website.

Conducting seminars and workshops is a way to get information about your book out there and you can sell your books to those who attend.

Many bookstores will provide a venue for you to do book signings.

The Internet provides a wealth of new opportunities to promote your book through Facebook and blogs. You can list your books on Amazon.com and other sites.


## SELF-PUBLISHING COMPANIES

If you do not wish to do everything yourself, you could use a self-publishing company, which is sometimes called a print-on-demand company. Some consider this vanity or subsidy publishing. You pay a so-called publisher for all the costs involved in publishing your book. Since you are paying them instead of them paying you for the right to publish your book, these are not really publishers; they are companies that are doing much of the work, except for the writing, for a fee.

You can choose from a menu of services that include editorial evaluation, page set-up, book cover design, and printing. Some also furnish editing services for an hourly fee. If your book is published under their company's name, you don't have to be concerned with things such as ISBNs, LCCNs, and bar codes. However, if the company gets your ISBN, it essentially owns the publishing rights to your book. If you want to truly publish your own book, you must get your own ISBN so that the book orders come to you, not to the self-publishing company.

These companies differ from each other in the services they provide. Don't expect these companies to be concerned about whether or
not your book is successful and makes a profit; they make their money
from the author who is paying them for their services. Some do a small
degree of promotion and many of them can get major book chains to
carry the books they produce. However, getting a book into a book
store means nothing if it doesn't sell.

Among some of the larger self-publishing companies are Xlibris,
AuthorHouse, Lulu, and iUniverse. Writer's Digest recently entered the
business. Since they all offer different services at different costs, it's best
to check them out yourself. Depending on what you want them to do
for you, the costs can range from several hundred dollars to upwards of
$25,000.

In general, the reputation of self-publishing companies is spotty.
Often the books look nice on the outside but unless the text has been
professionally edited, there can be many typos, misspellings, grammatical errors, and other mistakes. Before you decide to use one of these
companies, do some research. If possible, find authors who have used
them and can tell you what their experience has been. Be sure you
understand what you are getting into before you commit.

## Adjusting to the changing climate of publishing

The publishing industry, which includes books, magazines, newspapers,
and professional journals, seems to be heading in the same direction as
the recording industry. According to Forrester Research, revenue from
U.S. music sales and licensing was $14.6 billion in 1999. In 2009 it had
plunged to $6.3 billion. At the end of 1999 the music business was
worth half of what it was ten years before. The Recording Industry
Association of America (RIAA) has reported declining revenue during
this period with album sales falling about 8 percent each year. This is
mainly due to the volume of unauthorized downloads which continues
to represent about 90 percent of the market. There has been some con-

cern that e-books, like music, may become easy to download without paying for them.

The massive decline in both the book publishing industry and the recording industry has also been because of the growing popularity of digital books and music. David Goldberg, the former head of Yahoo! music says, "The CD is still disappearing, and nothing is replacing it in entirety as a revenue generator." By the same token, sales of paper and ink books have declined while e-books are growing by leaps and bounds. According to the Association of American Publishers, "e-books accounted for about 9% (in 2010) of sales for the major publishers." *Publishers Weekly* reported "Among bestsellers, the digital portion can easily top 30%." Digital sales at Random House reportedly spiked about 250% in 2010.

With all these massive advances in technology and the rapidity with which they occur, will they affect the work of the freelance editor? Most certainly. We will have to keep up with these changes if we are to survive in our chosen profession. Either we will have to keep abreast of the new technological climate or work in partnership with someone who does.

Depending on your point of view, the future looks exciting and promising or disquieting and foreboding. Either way, these are challenging times. As freelancers and entrepreneurs, we knew there could be times like these. However, as long as there are writers there will be a need for editors. And to paraphrase E. L. Doctorow (who was speaking of writing a novel), making a career of freelance editing is "like driving a car at night. We can see only as far as our headlights, but we can make the whole trip that way."

And what a beautiful trip it could be!

# *Resources*

## STYLE BOOKS

***The Associated Press Stylebook, 2010.*** AP Books. Edited by Darrell Christian, Sally Jacobsen, and David Minthorn. 450+ pages, ISBN 978-0-917360-54-1, 2010. A searchable web-based version is available for a $25 annual subscription. website: www.apbookstore.com

The *Associated Press Stylebook and Briefing on Media Law* is a spiral-bound manual. It is available in print as well as the Web-based Stylebook Online, providing fundamental guidelines on spelling, grammar, punctuation, and usage, with special sections on social media, reporting business and sports. Called "the journalist's bible," the AP's *Stylebook* is considered the essential tool for writers, editors, students, and public relations specialists. First produced in 1953, it was created partly because of a technical change in the way the AP transmitted news. It also provided a consistency in styles for a worldwide editorial staff that produced stories for newspapers. Major revisions have taken place over the past few decades and the print edition is now updated annually. The Associated Press is a global news network, delivering news from every corner of the world to all media platforms and formats. They claim to be the largest and most trusted source of independent news and information.

***The Chicago Manual of Style,*** **16th Edition.** Edited by University of Chicago Press Staff. 1,026 pages, ISBN 978-0-226-10420-1, August 2010. Website: www.press.uchicago.edu

The 16th edition is available in book form and as a subscription website. The same content from the *Chicago Manual* is in both versions. It includes free tools for editors and writers. Often called the "bible" of the book publishing industry, it is the authoritative, trusted source that writers, editors, and publishers turn to for guidance on style and process. Every aspect of coverage has been reconsidered to reflect how publishing professionals work today. It offers expanded information on producing electronic publications, including web-based content and e-books.

***The Chicago Manual of Style Online*** is available to individuals for a prepaid annual subscription of $35. Two-year subscriptions are also available for a discounted rate of $60. All subscriptions include access to the full contents of the 15th and 16th editions. Website: www.chicago-manualofstyle.org

***Concise Rules of APA Style,* Sixth Edition.** American Psychological Association. 284 pages, ISBN 978-1-4338-0560-8, July 2009. Spiral Bound. Website: www.apastyle.org

This provides writing and formatting standards for students, teachers, researchers, clinicians, and editors in the social and behavioral sciences. It targets only those rules writers need for choosing the best words and format for their articles and offers a comprehensive list of essential writing standards in a convenient, easily retrievable format. *The Concise Rules* contains a wealth of new reference examples with a focus on new electronic formats.

***The Elements of Style,* Fourth Edition,** William Strunk, Elwyn Brooks White, and Roger Angell. Allyn and Bacon 2000, 105 pages, ISBN 0-205-30902-X (paperback). ISBN 0-205-31342-6 (casebound).

*The Elements of Style* was originally a textbook written and privately printed by the author, William Strunk Jr., an English professor at Cornell University. "The little book," as Strunk himself called it, was required for use in his course called English 8. One of his students, E. B. White, discovered it in 1919. It was a forty-three page "summation of the case for cleanliness, accuracy, and brevity in the use of English" according to White. Several editions have been published through the years but it is the fourth edition with revisions, an introduction, and a chapter on writing by E. B. White that is widely used now. It remains an excellent resource for writers. The *New York Times* stated, "Buy it, study it, enjoy it. It's as timeless as a book can be in our age of volubility."

***MLA Handbook for Writers of Research Papers,* 7th Edition.** Modern Language Association. 292 pages, ISBN 9781603290241, 2009 (paperback). ISBN 9781603290258 (large print). Website: www.mla.org

Called the style bible for most college students, the *MLA Handbook* is adopted by universities, colleges, and secondary schools. MLA style for documentation is widely used in the humanities, especially in writing on language and literature. Generally simpler and more concise than other styles, it gives step-by-step advice on every aspect of writing research papers. The association's guidelines are also used by over 1,100 scholarly and literary journals, newsletters, and magazines and by many university and commercial presses. The seventh edition includes a guide to research and writing in the online environment.

***New York Times Manual of Style and Usage.*** Revised and expanded edition. Edited by Allan M. Siegal and William G. Connolly. ISBN 0-8129-6389-X. New York Times Books, 1999.

The official style guide used by the writers and editors of the *New York Times.*

***Publication Manual of the American Psychological Association,* Sixth Edition.** American Psychological Association. 272 pages, ISBN 978-1-4338-0561-5, July 2009. Available in softcover, hardcover, and spiral bound.

The APA *Manual* is described by the publisher as "the style manual of choice for writers, editors, students, and educators in the social and behavioral sciences. It provides invaluable guidance on all aspects of the writing process, from the ethics of authorship to the word choice that best reduces bias in language. Well-known for its authoritative and easy-to-use reference and citation system, the *Publication Manual* also offers guidance on choosing the headings, tables, figures, and tone that will result in strong, simple, and elegant scientific communication."

The *Manual* is the best source for broad background information about scientific publishing. It provides detailed guidance on publication ethics, journal article reporting standards, and the process of journal publication. The Sixth Edition contains new examples that have been drawn from publications in education, business, and nursing as well as psychology.

***Scientific Style and Format: The CSE Manual for Authors, Editors, and Publishers,* Seventh Edition.** Council of Science Editors. Hardcover 680 pages, ISBN 0-9779665-0-X, June 2006. $59.95; CSE Member Price: $47.95. Email: CSE@CouncilScienceEditors.org.

*The CSE Manual* is the most recognized, authoritative reference for authors, editors, publishers, students, and translators in all areas of science and related fields. The seventh edition has been updated and expanded to reflect changes in recommendations from authoritative international bodies. New chapters cover the responsibilities of authors, editors, and peer reviewers in scientific publication.

***U.S. News Stylebook: A Usage Guide for Writers and Editors,* 9th Edition.** U.S. News & World Report Inc. 224 pages, Spiral bound, $18.95. Website: www.usnews.com

The *Stylebook* covers the nuts and bolts of grammar, punctuation, and quotations as well as the sensitive issues of fairness, slang, gender bias, and more.


OTHER REFERENCES

***Books in Print.*** R. R. Bowker & Co., published annually

***Business and Legal Forms for Authors and Self-Publishers,*** Revised Edition by Tad Crawford, Allworth Press

*The Complete Guide to Editing Your Fiction* by Michael Seidman, Writer's Digest Books

*The Copyright Permission and Libel Handbook, A Step-by-Step Guide for Writers, Editors, and Publishers.* John Wiley & Sons, Inc.

*Editing Fact and Fiction, A Concise Guide to Book Editing,* by Leslie T. Sharpe and Irene Gunther. Cambridge University Press

*Forthcoming Books.* R. R. Bowker & Co., published annually

*Freelance Writers' Guide,* Second Edition, edited by James Waller. National Writers Union

*Guide to Literary Agents.* Writer's Digest Books, published annually

*Literary Marketplace.* R. R. Bowker & Co., published annually

*Manual for Writers & Editors: A clear, authoritative guide to effective writing and publishing.* Merriam-Webster, Inc.

*A Manual for Writers of Term Papers, Theses, and Dissertations,* Sixth Edition by Kate Turabian. The University of Chicago Press

*The Oxford American Dictionary of Current English.* Oxford University Press

*Random House Webster's Unabridged Dictionary.* Random House, Inc.

*Random House Webster's College Dictionary.* Random House, Inc.

*Screenplay: The Foundations of Screenwriting, A Step-by-Step Guide from Concept to Finished Script,* by Syd Field. A Dell Trade Paperback

*The Subversive Copy Editor: Advice from Chicago* by Carol Fisher Saller. The University of Chicago Press

*Webster's II New College Dictionary.* Houghton Mifflin Company

*Webster's New Universal Unabridged Dictionary.* Barnes & Noble Books

*Writers Encyclopedia,* Third Edition, from the Editors of *Writer's Digest.* Writer's Digest Books

*The Writer's Guide to Corporate Communications* by Mary Moreno. Allworth Press

*The Writer's Guide to Queries, Pitches & Proposals* by Moira Allen. Allworth Press

*The Writer's Legal Companion: The Complete Handbook for the Working Writer,* Third Edition by Brad Bunnin. Perseus Books

*The Writer's Legal Guide: An Authors Guild Desk Reference,* Third Edition by Tad Crawford and Kay Murray. Allworth Press, copublished with The Authors Guild

*Writer's Market: Where & How to Sell What You Write.* Writer's Digest Books, published annually

## PERIODICALS

*Library Journal.* 245 W. 17th Street, New York, NY 10011-5300

*Poets & Writers Inc.* 72 Spring St., New York, NY 10012 (bi-monthly magazine for literary writers and poets)

*Publishers Weekly,* a Cahners/R. R. Bowker publication (international news magazine of book publishing and bookselling)

*The Writer,* monthly magazine, Kalmbach Publishing Co., 21027 Crossroads Circle, P.O. Box 1612, Waukesha, WI 53187-1612

*Writer's Digest,* F & W Publications, 1507 Dana Avenue, Cincinnati, OH 45207 (monthly magazine)

## PROFESSIONAL ORGANIZATIONS

**Academy of American Poets.** 584 Broadway, Suite 604, New York, NY 10012-5243. (212) 274-0343. Fax: (212) 274-9427. Email: academy@poets.org. Website: www.poets.org

**American Booksellers Association** (ABA). 200 White Plains Road, Suite 600, Tarrytown, NY 10591. (914) 591-2665. Fax: (914) 591-2720. Email: info@bookweb.org. Website: www.bookweb.org

**American Medical Writers Association** (AMWA). 30 West Gude Drive, Suite 525, Rockville, MD 20850-1161. (301) 294-5303, Fax: (301) 294-9006. Email: amwa@amwa.org. Website: www.amwa.org

**American Society of Journalists & Authors** (ASJA). 1501 Broadway, Suite 302, New York, NY 10036. (212) 997-0947. Fax: (212) 937-2315. Email: director@asja.org. Website: www.asja.org

**American Crime Writers League** (ACWL). 17367 Hilltop Ridge Drive, Eureka, MO 63205. Website: www.acwl.org

**American Screenwriters Association** (ASA). 269 S. Beverly Drive, Suite 2600, Beverly Hills, CA 90212-3807. (866) 265-9091. Email: asa@goasa.com. Website: www.asascreenwriters.com.

**American Translators Association** (ATA). 225 Reinekers Lane, Suite 590, Alexandria, VA 22314. (703) 683-6100. Fax: (703) 683-6122. Email: ata@atanet.org. Website: www.atanet.org.

**Association for Women in Communications** (AWC). 3337 Duke Street, Alexandria, VA 22314. (703) 370-7436. Fax: (703) 342-4311. Email: info@womcom.org. Website: www.womcom.org

**Association of American Publishers** (AAP). 71 Fifth Avenue, 2nd Floor, New York, NY 10003. (212) 255-0200. Fax (212) 255-7007. Website: www.publishers.org

**Association of Authors' Representatives** (AAR). 676-A 9th Avenue, Suite 312, New York, NY 10036. (212) 840-5770. Email: administrator@aaronline.org. Website: www.aaronline.org

**The Authors Guild, Inc.** 31 E. 32nd Street, 7th Floor, New York, NY 10016. (212) 563-5904. Fax: (212) 564-5363. Email: staff@authors-guild.org. Website: www.authorsguild.org

**BioScience Writers.** 8418 Bluegate Street, Houston, TX 77025. (713) 516-1424. Fax: (713) 664-4597. Website: www.biosciencewriters.com

**Book Editing Associates.** Website: www.book-editing.com

**Council of Science Editors (CSE).** 10200 W. 44th Avenue Suite 304, Wheat Ridge, CO 80033. (720) 881-6046. Website: www.coun-cilscienceeditors.org

**EditAvenue Incorporated**. 4 Cypress Street, Unit 2, Brookline, MA 02445. Website: www.editavenue.com

**Editorial Freelancers Association.** 71 West 23rd Street, 4th Floor, New York, NY 10010. (212) 929-5400. Website: www.the-efa.org

**Education Writers Association** (EWA). 2122 P Street NW, Suite 201, Washington DC 20037. (202) 452-9830. Fax: (202) 452-9837. Email: ewa@ewa.org. Website: www.ewa.org.

**Freelancers Union.** 20 Jay Street, Suite 700, Brooklyn, NY 11201. Website: freelancersunion.org

**National League of American Pen Women** (NLAPW). 1300 17th Street NW, Washington DC 20036-1973. (202) 785-1997. Fax: (202) 452-8868. Email: nlapw1@verizon.net. Website: www.americanpen-women.org

**National Writers Association** (NWA). 10940 S. Parker Road, #508, Parker, CO 80134. (303) 841-0246. Fax: (303) 841-2607. Email: natl-writersassn@hotmail.com. Website: www.nationalwriters.com

**National Writers Union** (NWU). 256 W. 38th Street, Suite 703, New York, NY 10018. (212) 254-0279. Fax: (212) 254-0673. Email: nwu@nwu.org. Website: www.nwu.org

**PEN American Center.** 588 Broadway, Suite 303, New York, NY 10012-3225. (212) 334-1660. Fax: (212) 334-2181. Email: pen@pen.org. Website: www.pen.org

**Society of American Business Editors and Writers** (SABEW). Walter Cronkite School of Journalism and Mass Communication, Arizona State University, 555 N. Central Avenue Suite 302, Phoenix, AZ 85004-1248. (602) 496-7862. Fax: (602) 496-7041. Website: www.sabew.org.

**Writers Guild of America–East** (WGA). 555 W. 57th Street, Suite 1230, New York, NY 10019. (212) 767-7800. Fax: (212) 582-1909. Email: info@wgaeast.org. Website: www.wgaeast.org

**Writers Guild of America–West** (**WGA**W). 7000 W. Third Street, Los Angeles, CA 90048. (323) 951-4000. Fax: (323) 782-4800. Website: www.wga.org

# *Glossary*

**A**

**#9 envelope.** This, containing your name and address, can be sent along with an invoice for the client's convenience in sending in their payment. It is 3-7/8 x 8-7/8 inches and fits inside a standard business envelope.

**#10 envelope.** A standard business-size envelope, 4-1/8 x 9-1/2 inches.

**accordion fold.** A bindery term; two or more parallel folds which open like an accordion.

**acquisitions editor.** The person at a book publishing company in charge of acquiring product; usually the person to whom a query or book proposal is sent.

**active voice.** A voice of verbal inflection in which the subject of the sentence is represented as performing the action expressed by the verb.

**advance.** A sum of money a publisher pays a writer prior to the publication of a book. It is an advance against royalties, usually paid in installments of one-half at the signing of the contract and one-half upon delivery and acceptance of the complete manuscript.

**agent.** A person authorized to act on another's behalf. Agents are paid on a percentage basis, usually 15 percent for a literary agent representing authors of books and 10 percent for WGA (Writers Guild of America) agents representing script writers.

**alteration.** A change from the manuscript copy introduced in proof.

**antagonist.** A major character opposing the protagonist.

**Arabic numerals.** Digits used in arithmetical computation (1, 2, 3, 4, 5, etc.).

**artboard.** Alternate term for mechanical art.

**artwork.** Illustrations, such as photographs, drawings, maps, etc. intended for reproduction.

**assignment.** Given by an editor/publisher to a writer for a specific article or book for an agreed–upon fee.

**attachment.** A file included in a letter or embedded in an email.

**auction.** Publisher's bids for the acquisition of a book manuscript that is expected to be very successful. The bids include the amount of the author's advance, promotional expenses, and royalty percentage. Auctions are conducted by agents.

**author's corrections.** Changes and additions in copy after it has been typeset.

## B

**B2B: business to business.** A website that sells goods and services to other businesses.

**B2C: business to consumer.** A business that sells goods and services to the consumer.

**B2E: business to employee.** Communication between business and employee.

**B2G: business to government.** A business that sells to governmental agencies.

**backlist.** A publisher's list of books that were not published during the current season, but are still in print.

**back margin.** The inner margin of a page, along the binding side. Also called **gutter.**

**back matter.** Elements of a book that follow the text, such as appendix, index, glossary, list of resources, bibliography, and author biography.

**back up.** (Printing term) Printing the second side of a sheet already printed on one side.

**banding.** Method of packaging printed pieces of paper using rubber or paper bands.

**bar code.** A set of short, vertical lines and spaces printed on a product, designed to be machine readable to yield a price, ISBN, etc. Required by most retailers.

**bibliography.** A list of source materials such as books and articles used in the preparation of a book or referred to in the text.

**bind.** To fasten sheets or signatures with wire, thread, glue, or by other means.

**bindery.** The finishing department of a print shop or firm specializing in finishing printed products.

**binding.** (1) A covering for the pages of a publication. (2) The process by which the cover is attached.

**bleed.** Printing that goes to the edge of the sheet after trimming.

**blog.** Short for weblog.

**blueline.** Also called *blueline proof* and *blues*. A photographic proof generated by a printing firm from a typesetter's electronic files.

**blurb.** The copy on the back cover of a paperback or back cover of dust jacket on a hardcover book with promotional copy, brief author bio, or other information.

**body text.** The running text of a work.

**boilerplate.** A standardized contract.

**boldface.** Type with a darker, bolder appearance than standard type.

**bound galleys.** A prepublication edition of a book; also called *bound proofs*. Designed for promotional purposes; to be used as review copies.

**brightness.** The brilliance or reflectance of paper.

**browser, web.** A computer program designed to access information on the Internet.

**bulk.** Thickness of paper measured in number of pages per inch. The thickness of a publication including the cover.

**bundle of rights.** A copyright that provides authors, music composers, and creators of artistic works the sole right to grant or refuse permission to use their copyrighted works.

**burn.** Create a CD-R disk. In printing, it means to expose a printing plate to high intensity light or placing an image on a printing plate by light.

**butt.** Joining images without overlapping.

**butt fit:** Printed colors that overlap one row of dots so they appear to butt.

**byline.** Name of author that appears with the published piece.

# C

**caliper.** Paper thickness in thousandths of an inch.

**camera-ready copy.** Print-ready mechanical art.

**caps.** Abbreviation for capital letters.

**caps, small.** Abbreviation for small capitals.

**case binding.** A method of encasing a book in a rigid cover.

**cast coated.** Describes paper coated with a high-gloss, reflective finish.

**chapbook.** A small booklet of poetry, ballads, or tales.

**chapter book.** Small transitional books for ages 7 through 10 that help children move from early readers to full novels.

**character.** (1) A letter, numeral, symbol, or mark of punctuation. (2) A person represented in a drama, story, etc. (3) A part or role, as in a play or film.

**character count.** Measuring the approximate length of a manuscript by multiplying the number of characters and spaces in an average line by the number of lines in the manuscript.

**chrome.** A term for transparency.

**chronology.** Determination of dates and sequence of events; arrangements of events in time.

**CIP.** Cataloging-in-Publication; a cataloging record prepared to the standards of the Library of Congress which enables libraries to catalog titles.

**clips.** Clippings or samples from newspapers or magazines of a writer's published works.

**clothbound.** Book bound with a rigid cover.

**collate.** A finishing term for gathering paper in a precise order.

**color bar.** A quality control term regarding the spots of ink color on the tail of a sheet.

**color correction.** Methods of improving color separations.

**color filter.** A filter used in making color separations between red, blue, and green.

**color separations.** The process of preparing artwork for printing by separating into the four primary printing colors.

**comb binding.** Mechanical binding using a plastic, spring-like comb that fits through holes punched in the edges of pages.

**composite film.** Combining two or more images on one or more pieces of film.

**compositor.** See **typesetter**.

**content editor**. Person who evaluates the flow, logic, and overall message of a manuscript.

**continuity.** A continuous or connected whole.

**contrast.** The tonal change in color from light to dark.

**copublishing.** Arrangement where author and publisher share the costs and profits of a book. Also called *cooperative publishing*.

**copyeditor.** A person who does line-by-line editing to correct errors in spelling, grammar, consistency, punctuation, etc. Also called a *manuscript editor*.

**copyright**. A legal right granted to an author, composer, or artist for exclusive publication, production, sale, or distribution of a literary, musical, or artistic work for a specified period of time.

**cover paper.** A heavy printing paper used to cover books, make presentation folders, etc.

**critiquing service.** A service in which writers pay a fee for comments on their manuscript or book.

**crop.** To cut off parts of a picture or image.

**crop marks.** Printed lines showing where to trim a printed sheet.

**crossover.** Printing across the gutter or from one page to the facing page of a publication.

**cyan.** Blue; one of four standard process colors.

# D

**density.** The degree of color or darkness of an image or photograph.

**desktop publishing.** Creating and composing pages comprised of text and graphics on a computer.

**digital printing.** Printing with ink-jet or laser printers.

**digital proof.** A proof generated directly from electronic files, typically from a laser printer. See also **bluelines**.

**display type.** Type used for title pages, chapter headings, subheads, etc. See also **body text**.

**distributor.** A firm that stocks, promotes, sells, and distributes materials.

**drop cap.** An uppercase character set in larger type than the text and nested into lines of type. Usually the first character at the beginning of a chapter or other section of text.

**drop-out.** Portions of artwork that do not print.

**duotone.** A halftone picture made up of two printed colors.

**dust jacket.** Also called *jacket.* A protective wrapping with flaps that fold around the front and back cover of a clothbound book.

## E

**edition.** An original publication or any subsequent reissue in which the content is revised.

**electronic publishing.** The process of using a computer to enter both text and graphics and to integrate them for final output.

**em.** A unit of type measurement equal to the point size of the type in question.

**em dash.** A short typographical rule measuring the width of an em.

**emboss.** To press an image into paper so that it will create a raised relief.

**en.** A unit of type measurement half the size of an em.

**en dash.** A short typographical rule measuring the width of an en.

**end sheets.** The pages at the beginning and end of a book that are pasted against the inside board of the case; also called *endpapers, end leaves,* or *lining paper.*

**epigraph.** A quotation at the beginning of a literary composition that suggests the theme.

**epilogue.** A short concluding section at the end of a literary work.

## F

**foil stamping.** Using a die to place a metallic or pigmented image on paper.

**four-color process.** The process of combining four basic colors to create a printed color picture; colors composed from the basic four colors.

**flaps.** See *dust jacket.*

**flush.** Even, as with typeset margins. Lines that are set *flush left* are aligned vertically along the left-hand margin; lines set *flush right* are aligned along the right-hand margin.

**flyleaf.** A blank page at the beginning or end of a book.

**font.** A size and style of type. Also called *typeface.*

**foreword.** Part of the front matter of a book; a short introductory statement usually written by someone other than the author, often an authority on the subject of the book.

**front list.** A publisher's list of books that are new to the current season.

**front matter.** The elements that precede the text of a book, such as the title page, copyright page, dedication, table of contents, foreword, preface, introduction, and acknowledgments.

### G

**gallery.** A set of illustrations grouped on consecutive pages rather than scattered throughout the text.

**galley proof.** A proof showing typeset material without final pagination.

**genre.** A general classification of writing; a category.

**gloss.** A shiny look reflecting light.

**grain.** The direction in which the paper fibers lie.

**graphic novel.** A story in graphic form, long comic strip, or heavily illustrated story.

**gutter.** The two inner margins of facing pages in a book or journal.

## H

**halftone.** A tone halfway between a highlight and a dark shadow.

**hard copy.** A paper copy of a document as opposed to a digital copy.

**head margin.** The top margin of a page.

**highlight.** The lightest areas in a picture or halftone.

**hook.** Something that sets a work apart from others and draws interest.

## I

**idiomatic.** Peculiar to or characteristic of a particular language or dialect: *idiomatic expression*; having a distinctive style, esp. in the arts: *idiomatic writing.*

**imprint.** Name applied to a publisher's specific line of books.

**indicia.** Postal information placed on a printed product.

**infelicity.** Something inappropriate.

**infringement.** A violation, as of a law or agreement.

**introduction.** A preliminary part of a book leading up to the main part and written by the author. It may be extensive and is usually printed as part of the text.

**ISBN.** International Standard Book Number: the international standard numbering system for the information industry; required for books sold through bookstores.

# J

**jargon.** Specialized language of a trade, profession, or similar group.

**justified.** Spaced out printed lines so that left and right margins are aligned.

# K

**kern.** The part of a letter that extends beyond the edge of the type body and overlaps the adjacent character.

**kerning.** The adjustment of space between characters.

**kill fee.** A fee for an article that was assigned and then canceled.

# L

**LCCN.** Library of Congress Card Number; a pre-assigned card number issued by the Library of Congress. A unique identification number assigned to the catalog record created for each book in its cataloged collections.

**laminate.** To cover with film, to bond or glue one surface to another.

**landscape.** Having a greater dimension in width than in length. See **portrait.**

**layout.** A designer's plan of how the published material should appear.

**lead time.** The time between the acquisition of a manuscript by an editor and its actual publication.

**libel.** Defamatory statement.

**Library of Congress.** One of the major library collections in the world, located in Washington, DC and functioning as the national library of the United States though not officially designated as such.

**license.** Official or legal permission to do or own a specified thing.

# M

**magenta.** Red: one of four standard process colors.

**mass market.** Books that have wide appeal directed toward a large audience.

**matte finish.** Dull paper or ink finish.

**metaphor.** A figure of speech in which a term or phrase is applied to something to which it is not literally applicable in order to suggest a resemblance.

**middle tones.** The tones in a photograph that are approximately half as dark as the shadow area.

**midlist.** Titles on a publisher's list that are not expected to be big sellers but are expected to have moderate sales.

**moiré; moire.** Cloth with a watered or wavy pattern; odd patterns in photographs which occurs when screen angles are wrong.

# N

**narrative.** A story or account of events, experiences, or the like, whether true or fictitious.

**nonfiction.** All writing or books not fiction, poetry, or drama; the broadest category of written works.

**non-reproducing blue.** A blue color the camera cannot see. Used in marking up artwork.

**novel.** A fictitious prose narrative of considerable length and complexity, portraying characters and presenting a sequential organization of action and scenes.

# O

**orphan.** The first line of a paragraph stranded at the bottom of a page or column. See **widow.**

**overlay.** The transparent cover sheet on artwork often used for instructions.

**overrun or overs.** Copies printed in excess of the specified quantity.

# P

**page count.** Total number of pages in a book including blanks.

**paperback.** Bound with cover stock rather than a cloth-and-board cover. Also called *paperbound.*

**passive voice.** A voice of verbal inflection in which the subject of the sentence is the object of the action rather than causing the action.

**PDF.** An abbreviation for portable document format, an Adobe Systems file format for stable delivery of electronic documents, preserving the fonts, formatting, and pagination.

**perfect binding.** A technique for binding books by a machine that cuts off the backs of the sections and glues the leaves to a cloth or paper backing. Also called *adhesive binding.*

**perfect bound.** A book produced by perfect binding. Also called a **paperback** book.

**plagiarism.** The unauthorized use of the language and thoughts of another author and representing them as one's own work.

**plot.** Also called storyline; the plan or main story of a novel or short story.

**point.** The basic unit of type measurement—0.01384 of an inch.

**portrait.** Having a greater dimension in length than in width. See **landscape**.

**preface.** The author's own statement, often including acknowledgments. It follows the foreword if there is one and is part of the front matter of a book.

**prepress.** The process and preparation a printing company performs between the receipt of the electronic files and the printing of the publication.

**process colors.** Cyan (blue), magenta (red), yellow, black.

**protagonist.** The leading character.

**public domain.** Published material that is available for use without the need to obtain permission, either because it has not been copyrighted or has a copyright that has expired.

# Q

**query letter.** A letter, usually no more than one page long, in which a writer proposes an article or book idea; written to an agent or publisher asking for either representation or publication of the author's writing.

# R

**ragged left.** Type that is justified to the right margin with an uneven left margin.

**ragged right.** Type that is justified to the left margin with an uneven right margin.

**recto.** The front side of a leaf in a book or journal; in an open book, the page on the right; an odd-numbered page.

**remainders.** Copies of a book that are slow to sell and can be purchased from the publisher at a reduced price.

**reprint rights.** The rights to republish a book after its initial printing.

**roman numerals.** Numerals formed from traditional roman letters. Capitals: I, II, III, IV, V, etc. Lower case: i, ii, iii, iv, v, etc.

**running feet.** Copy set at the bottom of the page, often containing page numbers. In Word they are called *footers.*

**running heads.** Copy set at the top of a printed page, usually containing the title of the publication, chapter, author, or other information. Microsoft Word calls them *headers.*

## S

**saddle stitched.** A method of binding that uses thread or staples through the folds of gathered sheets. Often used in magazines and booklets.

**self cover.** Using the same paper as the text for the cover.

**shadow.** The darkest areas of a photograph.

**side stitch.** Binding by stapling along one side of a sheet.

**signature.** (Printing term) A sheet of printed pages which when folded become a part of a book or publication.

**silhouette halftone.** A term used for an outline halftone.

**Smyth sewn.** A method that involves stitching the signatures individually through the fold before binding them. A Smyth-sewn book will lie flat when open.

**specifications.** A precise description of a print order.

**spine.** The back center panel of a bound publication hinged on both sides to the back and front covers. The title, author, and publisher's names are printed on the spine so that the information can be seen when the book is shelved in a bookcase. Also called the *backbone*.

**stamping.** A term for foil stamping.

**stet.** A proof mark meaning to let the original copy stand.

**style sheet.** (1) A set of programming instructions that determine how a document is presented. (2) A record of terms kept by a manuscript editor to document particular usages for a specific manuscript.

**subhead.** A heading for a section within a chapter or an article.

**synopsis.** A general view; a brief narrative description of the book, usually one or two pages in length.

## T

**tabloid.** Newspaper format publication half the size of the regular newspaper page.

**tearsheet.** Page from a magazine or newspaper containing a printed story, article, poem or ad.

**theme.** An idea, point of view or perception.

**thesaurus.** A book of synonyms and antonyms.

**transition.** Passage from one subject to another.

**treatment.** In screenwriting, a synopsized narration of the story, action, and dialog, usually containing ten or more pages.

**trim size.** The dimensions of a full page in a printed publication, including the margins.

**typesetter.** A person who sets or composes type; compositor.

## U

**under-run.** Production of fewer copies than ordered.

## V

**verso.** The back side of a leaf in a book or journal; in an open book, the page on the left; an even-numbered page.

**vignette halftone.** A halftone whose background gradually fades to white.

## W

**watermark.** A distinctive design created in paper at the time of manufacture that can be easily seen by holding the paper up to a light.

**widow.** A short paragraph-ending line at the top of a page. See **orphan**.

**word wrap.** A word processing feature that automatically spills text from one line to the next without manually inserting line returns. Also called *wraparound*.

# Index

**Books from Allworth Press**

Allworth Press is an imprint of Skyhorse Publishing, Inc. Selected titles are listed below.

**Starting Your Career as a Freelance Writer, Second Edition**
*by Moira Anderson Allen* (6 × 9, 304 pages, paperback, $24.95)

**The Writer's Guide to Queries, Pitches and Proposals**
*by Moira Anderson Allen* (6 × 9, 288 pages, paperback, $19.95)

**The Author's Toolkit: A Step-by-Step Guide to Writing and Publishing Your Own Book, Third Edition**
*by Mary Embree* (5 ½ × 8 ½, 224 pages, paperback, $19.95)

**Publish Your Book: Proven Strategies and Resources for the Enterprising Author**
*by Patricia Fry* (6 × 9, 256 pages, paperback, $19.95)

**Promote Your Book: Over 250 Proven, Low-Cost Tips and Techniques for the Enterprising Author**
*by Patricia Fry* (5 ½ × 8 ¼, 224 pages, paperback, $19.95)

**The Birds and the Bees of Words: A Guide to the Most Common Errors in Usage, Spelling, and Grammar**
*by Mary Embree* (5 ½ × 8 ½, 208 pages, paperback, $14.95)

**The Writer's Legal Guide: An Authors Guild Desk Reference**
*by Tad Crawford and Kay Murray* (6 × 9, 320 pages, paperback, $19.95)

**Successful Syndication: A Guide for Writers and Cartoonists**
*by Michael Sedge* (6 × 9, 176 pages, paperback, $16.95)

**Marketing Strategies for Writers**
*by Michael Sedge* (6 × 9, 224 pages, paperback, $24.95)

**The Journalist's Craft: A Guide to Writing Better Stories**
*by Dennis Jackson and John Sweeney* (6 × 9, 256 pages, paperback, $19.95)

**Business and Legal Forms for Authors and Self-Publishers, Third Edition**
*by Tad Crawford* (8 ⅜ × 10 ⅞, 160 pages, paperback, $29.95)

**The Complete Guide to Book Marketing, Revised Edition**
*by David Cole* (6 × 9, 256 pages, paperback, $19.95)

**The Complete Guide to Book Publicity, Second Edition**
*by Jodee Blanco* (6 × 9, 304 pages, paperback, $19.95)

**Writing the Great American Romance Novel**
*by Catherine Lanigan* (6 × 9, 224 pages, paperback, $19.95)

**Making Crime Pay: An Author's Guide to Criminal Law, Evidence, and Procedure**
*by Andrea Campbell* (6 × 9, 320 pages, paperback, $27.50)

To see our complete catalog or to order online, please visit *www.allworth.com.*